Promises Kept
BECCA'S WINDOW

SHELLA K. FITZGERALD

Bloomington, IN  Milton Keynes, UK

authorHOUSE®

AuthorHouse™
1663 Liberty Drive, Suite 200
Bloomington, IN 47403
www.authorhouse.com
Phone: 1-800-839-8640

AuthorHouse™ UK Ltd.
500 Avebury Boulevard
Central Milton Keynes, MK9 2BE
www.authorhouse.co.uk
Phone: 08001974150

This book is a work of fiction. People, places, events, and situations are the product of the author's imagination. Any resemblance to actual persons, living or dead, or historical events, is purely coincidental.

First published by AuthorHouse 12/12/2006

ISBN: 978-1-4259-7985-0 (sc)

Library of Congress Control Number: 2006910513

Printed in the United States of America
Bloomington, Indiana

This book is printed on acid-free paper.

The scripture quotations in this novel are from the New King James Bible.

More fulfilled prophecy teaching can be found at www.eschatology.org

This book is dedicated
to all who are searching
for the truth of God's Word.

Thank you to Don Preston and the Ardmore Church of Christ
for their courage to stand for the truth
and for the encouragement they give to me.
Thank you to Ruth Ann McNeil for hours of editing.

Table of Contents

Chapter 1
An Afternoon Question

Becca awoke to the aroma of coffee drifting up from the kitchen. She pulled the covers over her head, willing herself back to sleep, but the empty sensation in her stomach persistently asked, 'Why fight it?' She laid the covers back and swung her feet gracefully to the floor. A gentle rain tapped lightly against the window pane.

Becca's room, an attic room, had only one window – a wonderful round window that gave her a view of the both the neighborhood below and the sky above. Her ceiling slanted in on both sides which often caused her to bump her head, but she didn't care. To her, the room, the ceiling, and the window were magical. It was as if the room didn't belong with the rest of the house. All the other rooms were traditional box shapes with flat ceilings and rectangular windows – no magic there.

The only other room in the house which had the slightest bit of magic was her grandma's room on the first floor. After Grandpa George died last year, Grandma came to live with Becca's family. Grandma's formal name was Mrs. George Alexander Elliott. She was especially proud of her name because she had been so proud of Grandpa. George Alexander Elliott, who had comported himself in a tall, straight, dignified manner, had been a respected and beloved minister of the gospel. Even though he had retired from active preaching in his later years, Becca could still remember going to hear Grandpa preach.

In Becca's memory, his voice echoed in the small country church where he had been the minister for forty years, "Won't you come to Jesus today? Repent of your sins, be buried with him in baptism, and rise to walk in newness of life. Won't you come today as we stand and sing?" The congregation would stand and sing *Just As I Am*. Sometimes he would stop the singing to make his appeal again, "Dear sinner, do not let this opportunity pass. Come to the Lord today, for we know not what tomorrow may bring. Christ will come with the sound of a trumpet when you least expect it. Will you not come to the Lord today?" Then the congregation would sing more verses of *Just As I Am*.

A large picture of Grandpa hung on the wall in Grandma's room. Grandpa's image lovingly smiling down on Grandma was just one of the treasures that made the room magical. Becca had once remarked to Grandma, "Look, Grandpa's smiling at you."

Grandma replied, "He is smiling at you, too, Becca." Then Grandma hugged Becca even harder than usual. Other pieces of memorabilia also made Grandma's room special. She had a matching mother-of-pearl brush and mirror set which had been a gift from Grandpa on their wedding day. Covering her bed was a beautiful quilt made from hundreds of pieces of cloth intricately set in a pattern which Grandma called *The Flower Garden*. Becca would listen while Grandma told her where each scrap of cloth had come from. Becca particularly loved the pieces which had come from her own childhood dresses.

Another of Becca's favorite things was the album filled with pictures of Grandma and Grandpa when they were younger, many of them with people Becca didn't recognize. Becca often wondered who all those smiling people were or what they were doing. She would occasionally ask Grandma about those people and listen intently to the stories from the past. But more than all the rest, Becca cherished Grandpa's Bible, tattered from diligent study throughout his life. Grandma kept it on the nightstand beside what would have been Grandpa's side of the bed. Often when Becca entered the room, she would find Grandma sitting serenely with her hand resting on his Bible, her eyes lost in visions of the past.

Becca pulled on her jeans, a sweatshirt, and her oldest pair of sneakers which Mom was threatening to throw away, gave her hair a quick brushing and started downstairs. She stepped quietly in case her brothers were still sleeping. The twins, Joe and Jim, were five years younger than Becca.

"Good morning, Sweetie," her mother greeted her as she entered the kitchen.

"Good morning, Sis," added Dad.

"Morning," Becca yawned in return. "What's for breakfast?"

"What do we usually have for breakfast on Saturdays?" her father chided teasingly.

"Pancakes," said Becca with a smile.

While Mom dropped the batter on the grill, Becca knocked on Grandma's door and peeked in. "Grandma, are you awake?" whispered Becca.

"Yes, dear, I'm awake". Becca knew she would be because Grandma was early-to-bed and early-to-rise.

"I brought you coffee."

"Thank you, Dear."

"Do you want pancakes?"

"No, just dry toast, thank you."

Becca set the coffee on the table, hugged her grandma, and pulled the side table closer to Grandma's chair before going back to the kitchen for the toast. There, buttering pancakes hot off the grill, were Joe and Jim, still in their pajamas with bed-head hair. They screwed up their faces as ugly as they could at Becca, who shot her ugliest face back at them. It was their way of saying 'good morning' without being too nice.

"Mom?"

"Yes, Becca," replied Mom.

"Can Jenny come over for a few hours today?" inquired Becca as the boys screwed up their faces at the mention of Jenny's name.

"Yes, this afternoon after the housework is done."

Becca made her ugly face back at the boys as she left with the toast for Grandma. "Please gather Grandma's sheets and laundry for me, Sweetie," Mom called after Becca.

After breakfast, Becca delivered Grandma's laundry and was in the process of gathering her own, which required her to dig under the bed in search of a missing sock. Instead of the sock, Becca found her Bible, complete with dust bunnies. A flush of shame shot through Becca at the sight of the neglected Bible. She had been avoiding her mother's inquiries each Sunday, 'Becca, are you not going to take your Bible to Sunday school?' Becca had offered excuses such as, 'We have some Bibles in our classroom,' or 'I think I must have left it at church last Sunday,' when, in truth, she didn't know where it was. Becca quickly wiped the Bible clean on her jeans, laid it on her bed, and continued to search for the missing sock.

The rest of the morning was filled with dusting, vacuuming (including the dust bunnies from under her bed), and folding clothes as they came out of the dryer. Finally, with all the beds made, the family sat down for a sandwich lunch. The rain had cleared earlier and Dad was planning to mow the lawn. While Mom was gone to the grocery store with her weekly shopping list, the twins went to their clubhouse behind the garage. When Jenny arrived at a little past two, the girls went up to Becca's room.

Earlier, when Becca had remade her bed with fresh sheets, she had moved her Bible to a soft upholstered chair. Becca had claimed the chair when Mom bought new furniture for the living room. She had lugged the chair up both flights of stairs by herself. It was into this soft chair that Jenny collapsed, pulling the Bible out from under her when she realized she had sat on something.

"Is this your Bible?" Jenny inquired.

"Yeah, just toss it on the bed."

Instead, Jenny unzipped the cover and read aloud, "To Rebecca Renae Elliott, June 2, 2002, from Grandpa George. Why June the second?"

"That's my birthday."

"Oh, yeah, I knew that. I just forgot," replied Jenny is an almost apologetic way. "Let's see, how old were you then?"

"Fourteen," answered Becca in a soft voice. "He gave me that Bible on the birthday that fell two weeks after I was baptized."

Jenny glanced up at the change in Becca's voice. "You OK, Becca?"

"Yeah, I'm sorry. I just remembered Grandpa giving me that Bible and my promising him that I would read it every day. Well, I don't.... but I should. This morning I found it under the bed covered with the dust bunnies; and I realize now that I haven't kept my promise to Grandpa. I miss him. I hope he doesn't know that I haven't been keeping my promise. He surely wouldn't be smiling down on me if he did."

"Smiling down at you? What do you mean?" Jenny moved over to sit on the bed with Becca.

"There's a picture of Grandpa in Grandma's room and it looks as if he's smiling down on you." Becca explained.

"Oh, I thought maybe you meant smiling down from heaven. You do believe that your Grandpa went to heaven, don't you? After all, he was a preacher, wasn't he?" Jenny hoped she was cheering Becca with thoughts of Grandpa in heaven.

After a moment, Becca, with tears in her eyes, turned to Jenny, "You know, I don't think I know for sure. Grandpa always preached that one day Jesus would come out of Heaven on a cloud, resurrect the dead, judge everyone, and, then, if you were judged to be good, I guess, then Jesus would take you home to Heaven. But since that hasn't happened yet, I don't know where Grandpa is." And then more slowly and thoughtfully, Becca said, "I guess he is in his grave." Stepping over to her window, Becca gazed up into the skies. The morning rain clouds had cleared, but evening clouds were gathering on the horizon. After a moment, she closed her eyes and rested her forehead against the cool windowpane.

Jenny could see that her attempt to cheer Becca had failed miserably, so. after several moments of silence, she made an effort to change the subject, "Hey, did you see who Sue was walking with at school last week?"

Becca welcomed the subject change and responded to Jenny's question. The rest of the afternoon was spent talking about school, trying on clothes, fixing each other's hair and nails and discussing other girl stuff. But silently in her heart, Becca renewed her promise to Grandpa to read her Bible every day. More importantly, she vowed to find the answer to her question: '*What happens when you die?*'

Chapter 2
Mr. Simms' Class

Despite the evening rains, Sunday dawned a beautiful fall morning. Walking with her family from the car toward the front of the church building, Becca saw Mike approaching from the other parking lot. She slowed her pace so that her timing accomplished two goals: her family went on without her and Mike reached the steps at the same time Becca did.

"Oh, hi, Mike," Becca said nonchalantly, as if she had just noticed him at that moment.

"Hi, Becca," Mike returned with a smile. Becca thought Mike had the most beautiful smile she had ever seen. Mike, a year older than Becca, was a freshman at the community college.

"Beautiful morning," Becca commented in an effort to keep the conversation alive. She paused at the door, hoping Mike would open it for her. He did. He is so wonderful, she reflected.

Members of the congregation greeted them as they entered the building. As Mike moved through the crowd and toward the hall to the educational wing, Becca lengthened her stride to stay by his side. Keeping up with Mike proved to be difficult because Mrs. Gardner stopped her to inquire about Grandma. Becca felt a little rude when she answered quickly, "She's fine," and hurried away before Mrs. Gardner could reply. She knew Mrs. Gardner would talk on and on, and Becca's main objective was to stay close to Mike. To her pleasant surprise, she discovered that Mike had waited for her.

As they continued down the hall, Mike smiled at Becca, saying, "Yes, it is a beautiful day." Mike had reached his classroom, the college age class, and was about to enter when he turned back to Becca and asked, "Are you going to the Fall Social tonight?"

Becca answered, "Yes," although she had not heard her dad mention if the family was going or not. She quickly reasoned that surely they would let her go even if they did not attend, because, after all, she was a senior in high school and it was a church activity.

"Great. I'll see you there," Mike said as he disappeared into the college classroom.

Becca's heart missed a beat. He had thought of her and a social function at the same time; but why, oh why, she fretted, simultaneously happy and disappointed, could he not have asked, 'Becca, would you like to go the Fall Social with me tonight?' Both happy and disappointed, Becca moved on to the high school classroom. As she took a seat beside Jenny, she caught a glimpse of Ben Wilson, a freshman who apparently had a crush on her.

"Hi, Becca," Ben's voice cracked as several people smirked or giggled.

"Hi, Ben. Hi, Brian," Becca said as she sat down. She had quickly added the 'Hi, Brian' so Ben would not think she had noticed just him. Behind her back, Brian had an amazed look on his face that asked, 'Why did she say 'Hi' to me?'

The teacher, Mr. Simms, entered the energetically room and beamed, "Good morning, everyone." A few class members mumbled back, "Morning." Mr. Simms was a fairly good teacher, but sometimes the forty-five minutes seemed like an eternity to Becca.

"Open your Bibles to Matthew 24. Today's lesson is about a discussion Jesus had with his apostles as they sat on the Mount of Olives. It is referred to as the *Olivet Discourse*." Mr. Simms called on different members of the class to take turns reading. They read all the way from verse one to verse twenty-eight before Mr. Simms said, "OK, let's stop there."

The Gospel of Matthew, chapter 24, verses 1-28:1 Then Jesus went out and departed from the temple, and His disciples came up to show Him the buildings of the temple. 2 And Jesus said to them, "Do you not see all these things? Assuredly, I say to you, not one stone shall be left here upon another, that shall not be thrown down."

3 Now as He sat on the Mount of Olives, the disciples came to Him privately, saying, "Tell us, when will these things be? And what will be the sign of Your coming, and of the end of the age?"

4 And Jesus answered and said to them: "Take heed that no one deceives you. 5 For many will come in My name, saying, 'I am the Christ,' and will deceive many. 6 And you will hear of wars and rumors of wars. See that you are not troubled; for all these things must come to pass, but the end is not yet. 7 For nation will rise against nation, and kingdom against kingdom. And there will be famines, pestilences, and earthquakes in various places. 8 All these are the beginning of sorrows.

9 "Then they will deliver you up to tribulation and kill you, and you will be hated by all nations for My name's sake. 10 And then many will be offended, will betray one another, and will hate one another. 11 Then many false prophets will rise up and deceive many. 12 And because lawlessness will abound, the love of many will grow cold. 13 But he who endures to the end shall be saved. 14 And this gospel of the kingdom will be preached in all the world as a witness to all the nations, and then the end will come.

15 "Therefore when you see the 'abomination of desolation,' spoken of by Daniel the prophet, standing in the holy place" (whoever reads, let him understand), 16 "then let those who are in Judea flee to the mountains. 17 Let him who is on the housetop not go down to take anything out of his house. 18 And let him who is in the field not go back to get his clothes. 19 But woe to those who are pregnant and to those who are nursing babies in those days! 20 And pray that your flight may not be in winter or on the Sabbath. 21 For then there will be great tribulation, such as has not been since the beginning of the world until this time, no, nor ever shall be. 22 And unless those days were shortened, no flesh would be saved; but for the elect's sake those days will be shortened.

23 "Then if anyone says to you, 'Look, here is the Christ!' or 'There!' do not believe it. 24 For false christs and false prophets will rise and show great signs and wonders to deceive, if possible, even the elect. 25 See, I have told you beforehand.

26 "Therefore if they say to you, 'Look, He is in the desert!' do not go out; or 'Look, He is in the inner rooms!' do not believe it. 27 For as the lightning comes from the east and flashes to the west, so also will the coming of the Son of Man be. 28 For wherever the carcass is, there the eagles will be gathered together.

Mr. Simms began, "Can anyone tell me what Jesus was referring to in verse two when He said, *'not one stone will be left on another'?*"

There was silence for a long moment before Jenny answered, "Well, verse one said they were looking at the buildings of the temple, so I guess the temple was going to be torn down."

"That's right. Thank you, Jenny." replied Mr. Simms with a smile.

Another girl asked, "Why are they going to tear it down? Are they going to build a better one?"

"No," said Mr. Simms as he shook his head. "Jesus is predicting here that the Temple was going to be destroyed. By the way, who worshipped at this Temple?"

Various people threw out possibilities, hoping to guess the right answer: "Jesus?", "The people?", "The apostles?", "The Christians?"

Mr. Simms extended his hands, palms outward, to stop the guessing. "Who were God's chosen people in the Old Testament?" he asked.

Becca held her hand up. She knew this one. "The Israelites."

"Yes, Becca. And who built the Temple for the Israelites?"

The guessing began again: "Moses?", "Abraham?", "King David?", "Peter?" Several people turned to look at the person who had said 'Peter'. Becca was at least sure that guess was incorrect.

Getting the class under control again, Mr. Simms decided not to ask any more questions. He continued, "At first, the Israelites worshipped at the Tabernacle until King Solomon, the son of King David, built the original Temple. Many years after Solomon's Temple was destroyed, King Herod built this Temple. Here in Matthew, Jesus is saying that this Temple is going to be destroyed, and, no, not to build a better one. I believe it was part of God's plan to destroy the Temple because it was time to leave the Old Testament Law and start following Christ and the New Testament Gospel. The Temple would no longer be needed."

When the class stared silently at Mr. Simms, he pressed on. "Beginning in verse four, Jesus tells his apostles that a time of tribulation is coming. Now, I believe the tribulation that Jesus is referring to happened in the first century. Some tribulation was inflicted on the early church by those Jews who would not convert to Christ. The Jews who thought it was wrong to believe in Christ persecuted the Christians. At the same time, the Romans, who ruled the world, also inflicted tribulation because they were trying to subdue a band of unruly Jews who were rebelling against Rome. Starting in verse sixteen, Jesus is warning his followers that, when they see all this trouble starting, they need to get out of Jerusalem because Rome is going to destroy Jerusalem and the Temple."

Becca had listened intently to all that Mr. Simms said. She had not heard this story before. "When did the Romans destroy Jerusalem, Mr. Simms?" she asked.

"I believe that happened in 70 A.D., Becca," answered Mr. Simms.

She further inquired, "Was Jesus still on earth when that happened?"

"No, no. Christ had ascended back into Heaven in about 33 A.D."

Mr. Simms talked on until the dismissal bell sounded and then hurriedly said, "Please read the rest of the chapter for next Sunday. It is about the Second Coming of Christ." Mr. Simms really didn't have much hope that the students would do the reading assignment, but he reasoned that it was right to encourage them anyway.

Becca watched for Mike as she and Jenny made their way to the auditorium. Most of the young people sat at the front on the right side of the auditorium. Becca thought that maybe, if she was lucky, she could slip in to sit next to Mike. Behind her, Jenny was saying, "Hang on, Becca. What's the hurry?"

Becca's efforts were to no avail. Mike was already seated in the middle of a row of other college kids, but she noted that at least there were boys on either side of him. Becca and Jenny sat on a pew two rows behind Mike. She tried to pay attention to the sermon, but her eyes kept drifting to the back of Mike's head. He had medium length brown hair that curled a little at his neckline. Mike and Becca had actually known each other since childhood but had not had much association with each other because they had not socialized in the same clique of friends.

Becca's attention snapped back to the preacher when she heard him say, "For the Christian, death is not something to fear. Those who die in Christ are with the Lord forever." What did he mean by saying, 'are with the Lord'? Didn't he mean to say, 'after the resurrection, they *will be* with the Lord'? But the preacher was through with his sermon and was offering the invitation.

The preacher's name was Dale Owens. He had been with this congregation for only two months. When he and his family had first arrived, Mom and Dad had hosted a dinner party for them to become acquainted with other members of the congregation, including Jenny's family. However, she and Jenny had retreated to Becca's room instead of staying downstairs with the adults.

After the worship service was dismissed, Becca looked for Mike outside the building but could not locate him. She said goodbye to Jenny and walked around the building to the family car. Her brothers were already there, quarreling over who would get the front seat. Dad ended the argument with, "All kids in the back seat and buckle up." They knew that would be the answer, but they liked to have the fight anyway.

As they drove home, Becca took the opportunity to ask, "Mom? Dad? Are we going to the Fall Social tonight?"

Mom replied, "Oh, is that tonight? Well, no, I wasn't planning to attend. Do you want to go, Dear?" her mom asked her dad.

"No, not if you don't want to," he said, shrugging his shoulders.

Becca ventured, "Well, I would like to go if it's all right with you."

Mom and Dad exchanged glances and agreed that it would be fine. "I don't mind taking and picking you up, Sis," said Dad.

"Thanks, Dad," said Becca with an exciting feeling swelling her heart. Then she remembered the preacher's comments.

"Dad? Mom? Another question," inserted Becca while she had their undivided attention. Mom turned her head toward Becca and Dad looked at her in the rearview mirror.

"Yeah?" He said with a question in his voice.

What did the preacher mean this morning when he said, 'For the Christian, death is not something to fear. Those who die in Christ are with the Lord forever'?" She was surprised that she had remembered it word for word. She continued, "He said, 'Are with the Lord'. Didn't he mean to say, 'Will be with the Lord after the resurrection if they are judged to be worthy'?"

Mom and Dad exchanged looks before Mom volunteered an answer. "I really think that is what he meant, Sweetie. He just didn't include all the details." Mom and Dad then exchanged those looks again. Becca did not understand what those looks meant.

Becca was satisfied with the answer but said in a lower voice, "Well, if that's what he meant, that's what he should have said." The rest of the ride home was quiet except for the twins relentlessly pestering each other. Becca wished they had a third row of seats so she could ride in peace away from two squirming twelve-year-olds.

At home, with clothes changed, the boys ran out to the backyard. Becca returned to the kitchen to help Mom prepare Sunday dinner, which was traditionally a full meal, not like lunch on other days. No one was in the kitchen yet, but Becca heard her dad from the hall say, "I think he meant exactly what he said."

"Surely not, Frank," protested her mom.

"That's what he has been saying in class, isn't it? That the Resurrection and Judgment happened in 70 A.D.," returned her Dad.

Her mom sounded frustrated, "Oh, I don't know. It's all so confusing."

As Dad entered the kitchen, he could tell by the look on her face that Becca had overheard what he said. "Sis," he said to acknowledge her and to signal his wife that Becca was present.

Becca did not want the topic to be dropped, so she interjected, "We were studying about 70 A.D. in our class today."

"Really?" her dad inquired, "What about 70 A.D.?"

"In Matthew…, Matthew…, I forget which chapter, Jesus said the Temple was going to be destroyed, and Mr. Simms said that happened in 70 A.D."

"That's right," said Dad with a sigh of relief. "It's Matthew 24." But Becca didn't let the subject drop.

"Did something else happen in 70 A.D.?" asked Becca as she looked Dad straight in the eyes.

Mom had entered the room and again Mom and Dad exchanged those looks.

Dad answered, "Oh, there are some scriptures that we have been studying in our class with Brother Owens. But I'm not sure about…"

Mom interrupted, "Now, dear, it's not really anything to talk about right now, is it? We need to start preparing dinner."

Becca let the discussion end there, but she planned to talk with Dad at a later time.

Chapter 3
Frank, I Wish You Hadn't

"Dad, are you busy?" asked Becca quietly as she approached where he was sitting in the porch swing reading the Sunday paper.

"Not too busy for my girl," said Dad, lowering the newspaper and making room for Becca to sit. "Is something bothering you?"

"Well, yes, a little. Yesterday, when I was talking to Jenny, I realized I don't know what happens to Christians when they die. I was thinking about Grandpa. Is he in the grave waiting for the Resurrection or where is he?"

"Well, Sis, a couple of months ago, I would have had a definite answer to that question; but, now, I am not sure."

"You're not sure?" Becca asked, bewildered that her dad, who was a deacon of their church, wasn't sure.

There was a brief silence while Becca tried to look into her dad's eyes, but his eyes were gazing off into space. Slowly, he turned to look at Becca. "Since Brother Owens came to be our preacher and also our teacher in the adult class, we have been studying some scriptures that I had never considered before. Some scriptures seem to be saying things that are not fitting into my understanding of God's plan, casting everything into a different light, if you know what I mean."

Becca did not interrupt, but nodded her head toward her dad as if to say, 'Go on'.

"Well, for instance, you said your class was studying Matthew 24."

Becca nodded.

"I had always been taught that the first part of Matthew 24 was prophesying the Destruction of Jerusalem in A.D. 70."

Becca had just learned about the Destruction of Jerusalem that morning, and she again nodded to encourage her dad to continue.

"And that the second part of Matthew 24 referred to the future Second Coming of Christ, you know, at the end of time." He paused for a moment before continuing, "But then I saw verse 34, which said it would happen in that generation. Jesus promised to return while those people to whom He was speaking were still alive. Jesus said, '...*this generation will by no means pass away till all these things take place*'."

"Do you mean the Second Coming of Christ happened in 70 A.D.?" asked Becca with her forehead wrinkled and her mouth gaping open.

"As I said, Becca, I'm not sure," answered Dad honestly.

"Well, we need to know – we need to be sure – don't we?" asked Becca still with a wrinkled forehead and a gaping mouth. Then, deciding it was too extreme to believe, Becca shook her head and said incredulously, "Dad, that's not possible. The Bible says, '*Every eye would see him*'. How could that have happened and we not know about it? If He has already resurrected the dead and taken them to Heaven, how are we going to get to Heaven? What about us, Dad?"

The front door opened and Mom stepped out onto the porch. "Frank, I wish you hadn't told Becca about this."

"Why? Why not tell me?" asked Becca, offended that she was being treated like a child.

Mom continued, "Sweetie, we don't want you to think we have not taught you the truth. We didn't want to shake your faith. Besides, I don't think that I agree with Brother Owens anyway. It is just too preposterous. Frank, this doctrine it is certainly not what your father preached!"

"Well, Elizabeth, whether my father preached it or not, I am going to study the issue. I want to know the truth. All scripture comes from God and I believe he intended for us to study and, hopefully, to understand it," replied Dad in a matter-of-fact way which indicated that his mind was made up.

Becca's mom closed her mouth and exhaled strongly out her nose, which was her way of giving up and getting the last word, too. Becca looked from her mom to her dad; then announced with determination, "I'm going to study, too."

"We'll study together," said Dad, putting his arm around Becca and giving her a bear hug that caused her to plead for mercy.

"Really, Dad, can I study with you?" asked Becca, a little bit amazed. "I mean, do you think I'm old enough to understand? After all, I'm only in the high school class."

Dad smiled, "Becca, you are an intelligent young lady, very responsible and mature for your age – and more than that, you are a Christian. I would be glad to study with you if you promise to take it easy on me."

Becca smiled back at her dad with a twinkle in her eye and asked, "Well, if I'm such a responsible and mature young woman, why do I have to ask permission when I want to go somewhere?"

"You don't," laughed her dad, hugging her again. "Just be sure to let us know where you're going, how you're getting there, who you're with, what you're doing and when you'll be home. Then, everything will be fine.

Becca bear-hugged her dad until he pleaded for mercy, "Hey, take it easy! I'm an old man."

Chapter 4
The Fall Social

Becca tried on three different outfits that afternoon before she was finally satisfied with her appearance. She was finishing her hair when Dad called up the stairs, "Becca, are you going to the Fall Social or not?"

"Coming," responded Becca grabbing her jacket, switching off the light and running downstairs. During the ride to the church building, Becca asked, "When are we going to have our first Bible study?"

"I want to get some books that might help us. In fact, I'm going to check some out of the church library tonight. So, how about Tuesday night, say about seven o'clock, after we help Mom clean up after dinner?" suggested Dad.

"Sure," smiled Becca.

Becca and her dad entered the fellowship hall from the side door. Dad went directly to the church library as Becca looked around, hoping to find Mike or at least Jenny. She spotted Jenny across the room talking, with a couple of other girls. As she made her way across the room, she became aware that someone was walking to the right and behind her. A quick glance told her it was Ben.

"Hi, Becca," Ben said when he knew that Becca had seen him. "I like your jacket."

"Uh, thanks," replied Becca over her shoulder as she continued across the room.

Ben continued, too, walking a little faster to keep up with Becca, "I was hoping you would come tonight. Uh, there are going to be some couples games later. Maybe you would be my partner?"

Becca stopped and turned to look at Ben. Ben had a hopeful, expectant smile on his face. "Yeah, maybe," answered Becca, surprised by his courage but also annoyed that he was following her. "Maybe," Becca said again as she offered a small but short-lived smile; then she turned to look for Jenny again.

Jenny and the girls had moved over to the refreshment table where a few boys were also gathered. Although Becca continued to make her way toward them, she became aware of someone walking beside her on the left. Assuming that Ben had moved around to the other side, Becca ignored the presence and kept her eyes focused on her destination.

Jenny saw her coming and greeted her as she joined the group, "Hi, Becca. Hi, Mike."

Becca shot a quick look to her left and there stood Mike, smiling at her. Then Mike took in the whole group, greeting everyone. Becca blushed faintly and said 'hello' to everyone and last of all to Mike. "Hi, I'm sorry. I didn't know that was you beside me."

"Thought it was Ben, didn't ya?" laughed Mike.

"Yes," admitted Becca, quickly checking to see if Ben was close enough to hear.

"Well, it's good to know you will have a partner in case there are any games that require couples," Mike added in a matter-of-fact tone.

Becca's expression hinted at a regretful embarrassed smile.

As she turned toward the table of snacks, Mike offered, "Why don't I get us a couple of soft drinks?"

Becca smiled and answered, "Sure. Thank you. Oh, make mine a Dr. Pepper if they have it."

"Hey, that's my favorite, too," added Mike. "Why don't you get us a couple of sandwiches and some chips and I'll meet you at that table over there?"

Becca and Mike arrived at the table at the same time.

"Hey, these look good," Mike said, pointing at the sandwiches Becca had chosen. Becca had chosen three half-sandwiches of different varieties for his plate.

"I didn't know what you liked. Oh, thanks," said Becca as she took the drink Mike extended to her.

"Yeah, these are great," said Mike, lifting the first sandwich to his mouth. He must have been really hungry, because his mouth wasn't empty for a moment until all three half-sandwiches were gone. Becca nibbled on a few chips. Mike noticed her sandwiches and asked, "Aren't you going to eat those?" nodding his head toward her sandwiches.

"Mom fixed dinner tonight. I've already eaten," explained Becca. As she lifted her plate toward Mike, he scooped up the two half-sandwiches. When those were gone, he leaned back to look around the room.

Becca felt nervous and wondered what to say to get a conversation started. Just when she had decided to ask Mike about college, she saw her dad approaching their table.

Dad smiled at Becca and then at Mike.

"Dad, you know Mike, don't you? Mike Gibbons," offered Becca.

"Oh, Mike. Yes, you're John and Linda's boy, aren't you?" asked Dad.

Mike stood up. "Yes, sir," said Mike, offering his hand. Dad and Mike shook hands. Before Dad released Mike's hand, he asked, "You started at the college this year, didn't you?"

"Yes, sir," answered Mike.

"How's it going?" continued Dad, releasing Mike's hand.

"Just great, sir," answered Mike. "Would you like to sit down, sir?" asked Mike, offering a chair to Mr. Elliott.

"Oh, no, no, no," replied her dad, gesturing with his hand that he didn't need a chair. "I just came over to ask Becca when she would like for me to pick her up," said Dad, looking to Becca for an answer.

Before Becca could respond, Mike interjected, "I would be glad to drop Becca off on my way home—that is, if it's OK with Becca."

Now her dad and Mike were both looking at her, each expecting an answer. Mike had just offered to take Becca home. Becca wasn't sure her heart was beating, but she smiled and managed to answer, "Oh, well, thanks, Mike. That will be fine with me. It will save my dad a trip. Thanks."

Her dad looked as if he expected more information, like possibly what time she expected to be home, but Becca didn't know what to say because she didn't know what time Mike planned to leave or when the Fall Social was scheduled to be over.

The silence was growing when Mike rescued her, "Will 10:30 be OK, Mr. Elliott?"

Her dad did not answer Mike, but looked at Becca, who now said, "I'll be in by 10:30, Dad."

"Great," said her dad, smiling at her before adding, "I think I found some books that will help with our study." Her dad gave the books a hopeful shake and then turned to Mike. "Thanks for offering to bring Becca home. I guess I had better get going."

As her dad made his way to the door, Mike sat down. He smiled, giving his eyebrows a lift that implied, 'typical dad'. Becca's smile and her face reflected the message, 'sorry about that'.

"What are you and your dad studying?" Mike asked.

"Oh, something from Matthew," Becca said, trying to dismiss the topic. She didn't know enough about the question or even about Matthew 24 to risk discussing it with Mike.

"Wow, a real Bible study?" asked Mike a little incredulously.

Becca thought he was making fun of the idea and answered back with a 'what's so strange about that?' tone in her voice, "Yes, a real Bible study. What's so surprising about that?"

"Don't take me wrong, but most people don't study the Bible. They just attend church and call it good."

Becca concluded that she must have looked at Mike with a blank or confused look on her face, because he confessed, "Well, to tell you the truth, I have never studied the Bible, outside of a Bible class, that is." Still Becca looked at Mike with no reply, so he continued, "Oh, I tried reading the Bible some, but it was pretty dry and I didn't understand much of what I read."

Becca had stopped staring at Mike and was staring at her plate instead. She decided to risk a little more information. "Well, I asked Dad a question about something Brother Owens said in his sermon this morning. And, well, Dad said that he wasn't, uh, …that he wanted to study that topic, too, and so we are going to study together on Tuesday night."

Even though Becca wanted to drop the topic, Mike pressed on with interest, "What question?"

Becca hesitated, staring blankly at Mike.

"Really, Becca, I'm not trying to make fun of you. Won't you tell me what your question is?" whispered Mike across the table, leaning closer to Becca.

Becca looked at Mike, then at her plate, and then at Mike again. She exhaled slowly and said quietly, "I was asking about death," she paused, "or, more accurately, what happens after death." Still leaning forward, Mike wrinkled his forehead, waiting for Becca to continue. In an I-don't-know-which-is-which voice Becca asked, "Does the Christian go straight to heaven, or does he have to wait for the Second Coming, the Resurrection and the Judgment?"

"What does Brother Owens have to do with it?" asked Mike, finally leaning back to his own side of the table.

"Well, this morning in his sermon he said that when a Christian dies he goes to Heaven, as if there was no Judgment," inserted Becca. "And Dad says that Brother Owens has been teaching some things like that in the adult class. Mom doesn't agree with Brother Owens, so Dad and I are going to study the issue."

"How do you start? Where do you start?" asked Mike considering the complexity of the issue.

"I think we are going to start with Matthew 24," said Becca.

"What's in Matthew 24?" inquired Mike.

"Jesus talking to his disciples about the Destruction of Jerusalem and the Second Coming," Becca whispered across to Mike. Now she was the one leaning across the table toward Mike.

"So?" said Mike as if that didn't have anything to do with the topic.

"So," returned Becca, "verse 34 says it would happen in that generation."

"Really?" said Mike, wrinkling his forehead, "*That* generation?"

"As I said, my dad and I are going to study together to find out what the scripture says or means."

Mike looked thoughtful for a moment but let the subject drop. They participated in a couple of group games. Becca even partnered with Ben in the three-legged race and with Jenny in the marshmallow passing game.

At about nine o'clock Brother Owens asked everyone to pull a chair in close or sit on the floor. After a couple of men had each read a short section of Bible scriptures, someone dimmed the lights and started a song. Becca enjoyed the songs they sang at these gatherings. They were less formal than the usual hymns they sang in Sunday worship. During the second song, Mike reached over, took Becca's hand, and held it until they were asked to stand for a closing prayer.

Mike again held Becca's hand as they made their way to his car. Becca was a bit disappointed to find that Mike had also promised rides to a couple of guys, but he did open the door for her to sit in the front seat. When he arrived at her house, she thanked him for the ride and let herself out of the car. Before the car door shut, Mike added, "Let me know how the study goes."

Becca said 'goodnight' to her mom and dad, who were watching TV in the living room, and went upstairs to her room. She stood for a while at her window, slowly brushing her hair. The night was clear and cool and the stars shown brightly above. She had enjoyed her time with Mike. It felt as if they were at the social together. She had not had to make an effort to stay near him because he was always close by, paying attention to her. He had held her hand. If only the ride home had been just the two of them.

Just then, a star shot across the sky and Becca made a wish. Then she got out her Bible and read Matthew 24. She read it carefully, three times through. Verse 34 definitely said that these things would come to pass in that generation. It included details about the sun being darkened, stars falling, Jesus coming on the clouds and the sounding of a trumpet. What she did understand about Matthew 24 is that it warned to be prepared, because no one knew when the Lord would come.

Becca moved back to the window. She looked at the beautiful stars above and closed her eyes in prayer to God. "Heavenly Father, help Dad and me as we study to learn your truth and to understand your Word so that we may serve you and please you. In Jesus' name, Amen."

Downstairs, Becca's dad and mom were saying a similar prayer together. Across town, Mike was reading Matthew 24.

The Gospel of Matthew, chapter 24:   1 Then Jesus went out and departed from the temple, and His disciples came up to show Him the buildings of the temple. 2 And Jesus said to them, "Do you not see all these things? Assuredly, I say to you, not one stone shall be left here upon another, that shall not be thrown down."

3 Now as He sat on the Mount of Olives, the disciples came to Him privately, saying, "Tell us, when will these things be? And what will be the sign of Your coming, and of the end of the age?"

4 And Jesus answered and said to them: "Take heed that no one deceives you. 5 For many will come in My name, saying, 'I am the Christ,' and will deceive many. 6 And you will hear of wars and rumors of wars. See that you are not troubled; for all these things must come to pass, but the end is not yet. 7 For nation will rise against nation, and kingdom against kingdom. And there will be famines, pestilences, and earthquakes in various places. 8 All these are the beginning of sorrows.

9 "Then they will deliver you up to tribulation and kill you, and you will be hated by all nations for My name's sake. 10 And then many will be offended, will betray one another, and will hate one another. 11 Then many false prophets will rise up and deceive many. 12 And because lawlessness will abound, the love of many will grow cold. 13 But he who endures to the end shall be saved. 14 And this gospel of the kingdom will be preached in all the world as a witness to all the nations, and then the end will come.

15 "Therefore when you see the 'abomination of desolation,' spoken of by Daniel the prophet, standing in the holy place" (whoever reads, let him understand), 16 "then let those who are in Judea flee to the mountains. 17 Let him who is on the housetop not go down to take anything out of his house. 18 And let him who is in the field not go back to get his clothes. 19 But woe to those who are pregnant and to those who are nursing babies in those days! 20 And pray that your flight may not be in winter or on the Sabbath. 21 For then there will be great tribulation, such as has not been since the beginning of the world until this time, no, nor ever shall be. 22 And unless those days were shortened, no flesh would be saved; but for the elect's sake those days will be shortened.

23 "Then if anyone says to you, 'Look, here is the Christ!' or 'There!' do not believe it. 24 For false christs and false prophets will rise and show great signs and wonders to deceive, if possible, even the elect. 25 See, I have told you beforehand.

26 "Therefore if they say to you, 'Look, He is in the desert!' do not go out; or 'Look, He is in the inner rooms!' do not believe it. 27 For as the lightning comes from the east and flashes to the west, so also will the coming of the Son of Man be. 28 For wherever the carcass is, there the eagles will be gathered together.

"Immediately after the tribulation of those days the sun will be darkened, and the moon will not give its light; the stars will fall from heaven, and the powers of the heavens will be shaken. 30 Then the sign of the Son of Man will appear in heaven, and then all the tribes of the earth will mourn, and they will see the Son of Man coming on the clouds of heaven with power and great glory. 31 And He will send His angels with a great sound of a trumpet, and they will gather together His elect from the four winds, from one end of heaven to the other.

32 "Now learn this parable from the fig tree: When its branch has already become tender and puts forth leaves, you know that summer is near. 33 So you also, when you see all these things, know that it is near — at the doors! 34 Assuredly, I say to you, this generation will by no means pass away till all these things take place. 35 Heaven and earth will pass away, but My words will by no means pass away.

36 "But of that day and hour no one knows, not even the angels of heaven, but My Father only. 37 But as the days of Noah were, so also will the coming of the Son of Man be. 38 For as in the days before the flood, they were eating and drinking, marrying and giving in marriage, until the day that Noah entered the ark, 39 and did not know until the flood came and took them all away, so also will the coming of the Son of Man be. 40 Then two men will be in the field: one will be taken and the other left. 41 Two women will be grinding at the mill: one will be taken and the other left. 42 Watch therefore, for you do

not know what hour your Lord is coming. *43 But know this, that if the master of the house had known what hour the thief would come, he would have watched and not allowed his house to be broken into. 44 Therefore you also be ready, for the Son of Man is coming at an hour you do not expect.*

45 "Who then is a faithful and wise servant, whom his master made ruler over his household, to give them food in due season? 46 Blessed is that servant whom his master, when he comes, will find so doing. 47 Assuredly, I say to you that he will make him ruler over all his goods. 48 But if that evil servant says in his heart, 'My master is delaying his coming,' 49 and begins to beat his fellow servants, and to eat and drink with the drunkards, 50 the master of that servant will come on a day when he is not looking for him and at an hour that he is not aware of, 51 and will cut him in two and appoint him his portion with the hypocrites. There shall be weeping and gnashing of teeth.

Chapter 5
No and Yes

Monday was fair and clear – a beautiful day. Becca and Jenny had senior English fourth period and afterward always ate lunch together. The cafeteria offered the standard school fare: cardboard meat, soupy mashed potatoes and smashed peas. After a few bites to appease their hunger pains, Becca and Jenny turned in their trays and crossed to the east entrance where they could sit on the steps and visit until their next class.

Jenny wanted to know everything about Mike. "Was that a date? What did you talk about? What happened when he took you home?" After filling in enough information to satisfy Jenny, Becca turned the conversation back to the topic of life after death.

Jenny, with a somewhat amazed tone in her voice, said, "Boy, Becca! You're really hung up on this death thing. I'm beginning to worry about you."

"I just want to understand. I want to know what the truth is." Becca paused for a moment, then continued, "Dad and I are going to start a Bible study tomorrow night. Would you like to come? I'm sure Dad won't mind." Becca looked at Jenny with a 'come on, pretty please' look in her eye, but Jenny shook her head.

"No, I don't think so." Then she confessed to Becca, "After our talk Saturday, I asked my dad about your question and he said that dead people go to *the land of the dead* until the Resurrection. And, well, that's good enough for me. I don't want to get bogged down in a study."

"What do you mean 'bogged down'?" asked Becca with a surprised look on her face.

"I just think the Bible is too hard to understand. One question will lead to another and you will never find the answers to all your questions. The study will be never-ending. That's why there are so many different religious opinions in the world. Just pick one and don't worry about it," concluded Jenny.

"Jenny, I can't believe you just said that. Don't you think God intended for us to know the truth?" Becca was looking intently at Jenny. Jenny shrugged her shoulders and started walking to her next class.

* * *

That evening, Dad handed Becca a book with a chapter marked in it. "Becca, if you have time, read this section before tomorrow night. Oh, yes, read Luke 17 starting with verse 5, also. It's a parallel passage."

"Parallel?" asked Becca, not understanding the terminology.

"Yes, that means there are two different writings about the same event. One is told by Matthew in his gospel and the other by Luke in his." explained Dad.

Becca still looked confused so Dad continued, "Matthew, Mark, Luke and John are called the Gospels. They all tell the story of Jesus and his ministry but are written by four different men from different viewpoints, so to speak. Matthew and Luke both have accounts of this same discourse Jesus had with his disciples."

Becca looked at the book Dad had given her. She didn't realize Dad was going to assign homework. As Becca thumbed through a few pages, the phone rang. Mom called from the hall, "Becca, it's the phone for you – some boy named Ben."

"Oh, no," moaned Becca as she made her way to the phone. She lifted the receiver from the hall table and said flatly, "Hello, this is Becca."

"Hi, Becca. It's me, Ben," said the voice on the other end. There was a moment of silence so Ben continued, "How are you?"

"I'm fine, Ben," answered Becca. Again there was silence. Becca knew she was not being very cordial to Ben, but she really did not want to encourage him in any way.

"Well," continued Ben. "I thought maybe you might like to go to a movie…with me, I mean…would you like to go to a movie with me?"

Becca could see that Ben was serious. She decided the best approach would be to be honest with him.

"Ben," began Becca. "I think you are a really nice guy. But, Ben, you are in the ninth grade and I am a senior. Let me tell you something about girls, Ben: they almost never, I mean never, date guys who are younger than they are. I appreciate that you like me, but the most that we can be is just friends." Becca repeated, "Just friends, Ben."

There was silence on the other end, so Becca continued. "Someday you will see a girl in your grade or even maybe a year or two younger than you and you won't even remember me."

Becca waited and she could hear the hurt in his voice when Ben finally responded, "OK, then. Bye." Becca heard the phone click off. She climbed the stairs to her room and had just settled into her chair to do a reading assignment for American Government, when the phone rang again. Mom called up the stairs, "Becca, it's the phone for you – some boy named Mike."

Becca dashed down the stairs. As she reached for the phone, she caught a glimpse of Dad in the kitchen. He gave her a quick wink as she said, "Hello, this is Becca."

"Hi, Becca, this is Mike. How are you doing?"

"Hi, Mike, I'm fine and you?"

"Yeah, I'm OK. Hey, we had a good time last night. Didn't we?"

"Yes, I really enjoyed it."

"Becca?"

"Yes."

"You know that Bible study that you and your dad are planning?"

"Yes"

"Well, I was wondering, if it's all right with you and your dad, do you think I could join you? I read Matthew 24 last night and I would really like to know what it is talking about. You're right; it said, '*in that generation*'. That blew me away. Do you think it will be all right if I come over for the Bible study?

"Oh," said Becca a little bit surprised and a little bit confused. Questions raced through her head. Would she be able to think or study with Mike present? Would she be too shy to talk? She knew Mike was waiting for an answer, so she said, "Just a minute, Mike. I'll ask Dad." Still not knowing how she felt about the idea of Mike's sitting in on the Bible study, Becca went to the living room, explained to Dad that Mike wanted to join their Bible study, and asked if he minded.

As Dad looked at Becca, his eyebrows went up and a smile brightened his face, "Sure, Sis, I think we could handle one more. What do you think?"

Becca said, "Yeah, I guess it would be all right."

Becca returned to the phone, inquiring, "Are you there, Mike?"

"Yes, I'm still here."

"Dad said it would be fine?" volunteered Becca.

"Is it all right with you? I mean, I won't come if you don't want me to."

Concerned that Mike had heard the nervous doubt in her voice, Becca tried to sound more confident, "Oh, yes, it's fine with me. It will be great."

"What time?" asked Mike.

"Oh, seven o'clock, yeah, seven o'clock," said Becca repeating herself.

"OK, I'll see you then."

Mike sounded as if he was ending the call. Becca came to her senses and interjected, "Oh, and Mike."

"Yeah?"

"Read Luke 17, starting with verse 5, I think: it's a parallel passage."

"Thanks. I'll see you tomorrow night then." Becca said a quick goodbye and Mike was gone.

She went back into the living room and sat on the sofa. She assumed she must have had a puzzled look on her face because Dad asked if she was OK.

"I'm OK. I'm just really surprised. Today, I asked Jenny if she would join our study, but she wasn't interested. She even said it was a 'waste of time', so to speak. That really surprised me and now Mike calls and he wants to come. I'm just confused."

Dad thought a moment, then said, "That does surprise me about Jenny, but I'm pleased that Mike is interested. He seems to be a really nice young man." Dad lifted the newspaper in front of his face before Becca could see the really big smile that was on his face. Dad was thinking 'Becca has a boyfriend'.

Before climbing into bed, Becca stood at her window for a while. A few clouds were flying past the moon and below her window the treetops were swaying gently in the breeze. She made a mental note to bake cookies for tomorrow night and to ask Mom to arrange for the twins stay in their room. After the American Government reading assignment was finished, Becca turned in her Bible to Luke 17. She read it through twice and then opened the book her dad had given her. It was a commentary on the *Olivet Discourse*. Becca remembered from Sunday school class, that Mr. Simms had called Matthew 24 the *Olivet Discourse*. Becca read the passage carefully and was surprised about half-way through when the author stated, 'Clearly, Jesus taught that He would return in that generation'. The author, however, concluded that Jesus had not accomplished what He had intended to do.

With these confusing thoughts about Jesus not doing what He had intended and thoughts about Mike coming to her house tomorrow night, the hour was late before Becca was able to fall asleep.

The Gospel of Luke, chapter 21, verses 5-36:   5 Then, as some spoke of the temple, how it was adorned with beautiful stones and donations, He said, 6 "These things which you see — the days will come in which not one stone shall be left upon another that shall not be thrown down."

7 So they asked Him, saying, "Teacher, but when will these things be? And what sign will there be when these things are about to take place?"

8 And He said: "Take heed that you not be deceived. For many will come in My name, saying, 'I am He,' and, 'The time has drawn near.' Therefore do not go after them.   9 But when you hear of wars and commotions, do not be terrified; for these things must come to pass first, but the end will not come immediately."

10 Then He said to them, "Nation will rise against nation, and kingdom against kingdom.   11 And there will be great earthquakes in various places, and famines and pestilences; and there will be fearful sights and great signs from heaven.   12 But before all these things, they will lay their hands on you and persecute you, delivering you up to the synagogues and prisons. You will be brought before kings and rulers for My name's sake.   13 But it will turn out for you as an occasion for testimony.   14 Therefore settle it in your hearts not to meditate beforehand on what you will answer;   15 for I will give you a mouth and wisdom which all your adversaries will not be able to contradict or resist.   16 You will be betrayed even by parents and brothers, relatives and friends; and they will put some of you to death.   17 And you will be hated by all for My name's sake.   18 But not a hair of your head shall be lost.   19 By your patience possess your souls.

20 "But when you see Jerusalem surrounded by armies, then know that its desolation is near.   21 Then let those who are in Judea flee to the mountains, let those who are in the midst of her depart, and let not those who are in the country enter her. 22 For these are the days of vengeance, that all things which are written may be fulfilled. 23 But woe to those who are pregnant and to those who are nursing babies in those days! For there will be great distress in the land and wrath upon this people. 24 And they will fall by the edge of the sword, and be led away captive into all nations. And Jerusalem will be trampled by Gentiles until the times of the Gentiles are fulfilled.

25 "And there will be signs in the sun, in the moon, and in the stars; and on the earth distress of nations, with perplexity, the sea and the waves roaring; 26 men's hearts failing them from fear and the expectation of those things which are coming on the earth, for the powers of the heavens will be shaken. 27 Then they will see the Son of Man coming in a cloud with power and great glory. 28 Now when these things begin to happen, look up and lift up your heads, because your redemption draws near."

29 Then He spoke to them a parable: "Look at the fig tree, and all the trees. 30 When they are already budding, you see and know for yourselves that summer is now near. 31 So you also, when you see these things happening, know that the kingdom of God is near. 32 Assuredly, I say to you, this generation will by no means pass away till all things take place. 33 Heaven and earth will pass away, but My words will by no means pass away.

34 "But take heed to yourselves, lest your hearts be weighed down with carousing, drunkenness, and cares of this life, and that Day come on you unexpectedly. 35 For it will come as a snare on all those who dwell on the face of the whole earth. 36 Watch therefore, and pray always that you may be counted worthy to escape all these things that will come to pass, and to stand before the Son of Man."

Chapter 6
Tuesday Night Number One

Tuesday, after school, Becca gave the living room and kitchen a quick cleaning. She wanted things to be as nearly perfect as possible for Mike's visit to her home. She even swept off the front porch. She discovered that her mom had already baked cookies and stocked the refrigerator with soft drinks. Becca set out a couple of cinnamon scented candles to light after supper to make the house smell really good. She had already brought her Bible and the commentary that Dad had given to her down to the kitchen. She placed the books on the clean counter with a supply of writing paper and freshly sharpened pencils.

Mom had prepared an easy casserole that was timed to be ready as soon as Dad returned home from work.

"Did everyone have a good day?" asked Dad as the family sat down to eat. No one answered, so Mom replied for everyone.

"Yes, Dear. I believe everyone is fine. Grandma said she was a little tired, so she is having a bowl of oatmeal in her room." With a laugh, Mom said, "I don't think she liked the look of my casserole." Speaking to the boys, Mom continued, "Joe, Jim, your dad is going have a Bible study here in the kitchen tonight, so you will need to stay in your bedroom and not make too much of a ruckus." Both boys looked as if they were being punished, but Mom cheered them up when she said, "I baked some cookies today, so I'll bring you a plate of cookies and some milk later."

They were satisfied, but, as if they knew the Bible study was Becca's fault, they made their ugly faces at her and she promptly made one back at them. Mom calmly remarked, "One of these days your faces are going to freeze like that." The boys and Becca both looked surprised; they didn't realize Mom had caught them at their ugly face game. Dad gave a little chuckle.

Dinner had just been cleared away and the boys banished to their room when the doorbell rang. Becca hurried to answer the door. "Hi, Mike, please come in."

Dad had also made his way to the front door and extended his hand to Mike. "Mike, it is good to see you. I'm so glad you wanted to join us tonight."

"Thank you for allowing me come, Mr. Elliott," answered Mike.

Becca led the way to the kitchen, saying, "I hope you don't mind if we study in the kitchen. It's the best place to spread out our books and papers." Becca had already laid out a couple of sheets of paper and a sharp pencil at three places where she intended them to sit.

As Dad took his usual chair and Mike and Becca were sitting down, Mom entered the kitchen, carrying her Bible. "I hope you don't mind if I join you," she said, taking a seat. Dad smiled as Becca got paper and a pencil for Mom. Mike stood and said, "Good evening, Mrs. Elliott."

Her dad jumped in with an introduction. "Elizabeth, you know Mike Gibbons, don't you? Frank and Linda's boy."

"Oh, yes. Good evening, Mike," returned her mom.

Becca was thankful when her dad took the lead. "Did everyone have a chance to read both Matthew 24 and Luke 17?"

All indicated that they had read the passages.

"Well, I'll start off with what I had always been taught. Mike, I don't know if you are aware that my dad was a gospel preacher for almost forty years. What he taught was that in Matthew 24, verses 3-14, Jesus is talking about the great tribulation that would happen before the Second Coming of Christ. See how verses 6, 13, and 14 all mention 'the end', which my dad taught meant the end of the world or the end of time at the Second Coming." Dad waited while they all read these verses silently. "And then, in verses 15-28, Jesus is talking specifically about the destruction of Jerusalem and how the disciples should flee Jerusalem and Judea to escape the danger. He said it will be particularly hard on women and children." The group quickly scanned those verses and again looked to Frank. "Then, in verse 29, Jesus changes the topic as He describes His Second Coming. He will come on the clouds with the sounding of a trumpet and will gather the faithful to take them home to Heaven." Everyone sat silently looking at him. Mom and Mike both seemed satisfied with his explanation. "And the rest of Matthew 24 continues to talk about the Second Coming of Christ – about how no one knows when it will be. Look at verse 36, '*But of that day and hour no one knows, not even the angels of heaven....*'." They all continued to look at Frank in silence.

He addressed Becca, trying to draw her out so that he wouldn't be the only one talking. "Becca, do you see a problem with what I said?"

Becca glanced at Mike, but he appeared to be reading, so she summoned her courage and said, "What I don't understand is in verses 32-35. It seems to be saying that the events He was talking about were near – 'at the doors' – in verse 33 and that 'all these things' would happen in that generation."

Mom inserted, "Well, the Destruction of Jerusalem did happened in that generation … in the year 70 A.D."

Becca did not want to disagree with her mom, but this was a Bible study and she had a question. "Yes, but, it says *all* these things, and part of the things He had been speaking about was the Second Coming. It sounds to me as if both the Destruction of Jerusalem and the Second Coming were to happen in that generation."

Mom again said, "Yes, all these things would happen in that generation, *but* of the Second Coming no one knows when that will be. He made an exception about the Second Coming." Mom looked hopeful and Mike nodded his head in agreement.

Dad took the lead back, "So, let's look at Luke 17. Hold your place in Matthew 24 and turn to Luke 17, also." When everyone had located both passages, Dad said, "I suggest we compare what Jesus said in the accounts of both Matthew and Luke. When you find verses in Matthew and Luke that are talking about the same thing, put the Matthew verse on the left side of your paper and the corresponding verse from Luke beside it to the right. Does everyone understand?"

Mike answered, "Yes, sir," and they all began to work except Mom, who left to check on the boys. She took cookies and milk to Joe and Jim, who were playing a video game. Becca stood, saying, "Would anyone like something to drink?" She got soft drinks for everyone.

"Oh, thank you," said Mike with a smile as Becca set the drink before him. Mom placed a plate of cookies on their table, too, as the comparison work continued. After everyone had made their lists, Dad suggested that one person make a master list, keeping the verses in order as they appear in the text. Becca got a piece of poster board and volunteered to do the printing. She listed the Matthew verses in order on the left side of the paper and listed the Luke verses in order on the right side, then high-lighted the passages that Dad said were talking about the Second Coming.

(1) Matt 24:17-18   Let him which is on the housetop not come down to take any thing out of his house: Neither let him which is in the field return back to take his clothes.

(2) Matt 24:23 Then if any man shall say unto you, Lo, here is Christ, or there; believe it not.

(3) **Matt 24:27   For as the lightning cometh out of the east, and shineth even unto the west; so shall also the coming of the Son of Man be.**

(4) Matt 24:28 For wheresoever the carcass is, there will the eagles be gathered together.

(5) Matt 24:34 Verily I say unto you, This generation shall not pass, till all these things be fulfilled.

(6) **Matt 24:37-38   But as the days of Noah were, so shall also the coming of the Son of man be. For as in the days that were before the flood they were eating and drinking, marrying and giving in marriage, until the day that Noah entered into the ark,**

(7) **Matt 24:39 And knew not until the flood came, and took them all away; so shall also the coming of the Son of Man be.**

(8) **Matt 24:40-41 Then shall two be in the field; the one shall be taken, and the other left. Two women shall be grinding at the mill; the one shall be taken, and the other left.**

(2) <u>Luke 17:23</u> And they shall say to you, See here; or, see there: go not after them, nor follow them.

(3) **<u>Luke 17:24</u> For as the lightning, that lighteneth out of the one part under heaven, shineth unto the other part under heaven; so shall also the Son of Man be in His day.**

(5) <u>Luke 17:25</u> But first He must suffer many things, and be rejected of this generation.

(6) **<u>Luke 17:26-27</u> And as it was in the days of Noah, so shall it be also in the days of the Son of Man. They did eat, they drank, they married wives, they were given in marriage, until the day that Noah entered into the ark, and the flood came, and destroyed them all.**

(7) **<u>Luke 17:30</u> Even thus shall it be in the day when the Son of Man is revealed.**

(1) <u>Luke 17:31</u> In that day, he which shall be upon the housetop, and his goods in the house, let him not come down to take it away: and he that is in the field, let him likewise not return back.

(8) **<u>Luke 17:35-36</u> Two women shall be grinding together; the one shall be taken, and the other left. Two men shall be in the field; the one shall be taken, and the other left.**

(4) <u>Luke 17:37</u> And they answered and said unto him, Where, Lord? And he said unto them, "Wherever the body is, there the eagles will be gathered together."

Dad continued, "Now, if the way I divided the verses in Matthew was correct, are the corresponding verses in Luke arranged the same way?"

They all looked from the chart, back to Matthew and back to Luke, checking to see if they had made a mistake or possibly missed something. Becca was the first to state the problem. "It looks to me as if Luke treats these statements as one topic, but is he referring to the Destruction of Jerusalem or to the Second Coming? Otherwise, he keeps jumping back and forth between the topics."

Mom checked her watch, "Oh dear, it is already 8:30. I've things I must prepare for tomorrow and the boys need to be put to bed," she said as she looked to Frank to agree with her.

"That's fine," said Frank in agreement with Beth. "Let's agree on a time to meet next. Also, I have some more passages for us to study." Everyone made a note of the study suggestions: Luke 21:20-36 and I Thessalonians 4:13-5:11. They agreed to meet next Tuesday night at 7:00.

As Mike was gathering his Bible and papers, Mrs. Elliott cleared away the refreshments. Mike said, "Goodnight, Mrs. Elliott. Thank you for the soft drink and cookies." Then to Mr. Elliott, he offered, "Thank you, sir, for studying with us."

Becca's dad smiled at both Mike and Becca as he said to Mike, "Well, Mike, please understand that I don't have all the answers. I'm studying just as you are, so please speak up when you have something to ask or add to the discussion."

Mike nodded, realizing he had not asked or added much tonight. "Yes, sir. Well, goodnight," Mike said as he turned to go.

Becca led the way to the door, and followed Mike onto the porch, pulling the door closed behind her. On the porch, Mike turned to face Becca and said, "You have a nice family."

"Thanks," responded Becca.

Mike continued with a little bit of a tease in his voice, "Did you find an answer to your question yet?"

Becca laughed, "No. I just found more questions."

"Yeah, me too," returned Mike, sharing the laugh. "Well, goodnight, Becca. I guess I'll see you Sunday."

"Yeah, see you Sunday," said Becca as Mike went to his car. She turned to enter the house but discovered that she had locked herself out. She waved at Mike until his car disappeared down the street before ringing the doorbell.

From the other side of the door, Becca heard her dad's voice mocking her, "Who is it?"

"Dad, let me in, please," said Becca in a voice that said 'OK, the joke's on me'.

Becca's dad opened the door with a big grin on his face. Becca spontaneously gave her dad her ugly face, then a smile, and a kiss on his cheek. Becca gathered up her Bible and papers and bounded up the stairs.

The view out of her window was beautiful. The trees rustled with the slight breeze and the street lights made each house look like a pleasant little scene. Stars twinkled overhead as Becca made a wish on the evening star. She was glad she was getting to know Mike, but she wondered if she dared hope that they would be more than just friends.

Chapter 7
The Afternoon Sun

On Thursday afternoons, Becca's mom served as a volunteer at the local hospital, so Becca always came straight home after school to be at the house with the twins and Grandma. The twins had already eaten a snack and were outside playing. In about an hour, Becca would call them in to do their homework. Becca always enjoyed her special time with Grandma every Thursday afternoon and she knew how much Grandma looked forward to these visits, also.

Becca made a tray of hot tea and cookies for Grandma and herself to enjoy as they chatted.

"Hello, Becca Dear," said Grandma sweetly.

"Hi, Grandma," said Becca as she bent down to hug and kiss her.

"Becca, is that sunshine I see on the back porch?" asked Grandma.

Becca replied, "Yes it is; let me check." She knew Grandma loved to sit on the porch whenever she could. Now that the days were turning cooler, Becca had to make certain that the weather conditions would be all right for Grandma, not too cool or too breezy. After Becca arranged the porch furniture for Grandma and herself to have an intimate visit, she stepped back inside, saying, "I think the porch will be fine for a while, Grandma. Let me help you." Becca offered her arm to Grandma.

As they made their way slowly to the back porch, Grandma commented, "I haven't been feeling very well for a couple of days. I think the sunshine will do me some good." After Grandma was settled in a chair, Becca brought their tea and cookies. She also picked up a lap blanket for Grandma. She set the tray on the table and offered the lap blanket to Grandma.

"I don't think I need that, Becca, but thank you for bringing it. I might need it in a little while," said Grandma.

They enjoyed their hot tea for a few minutes while the twins yelled for Grandma to watch as they performed some gymnastic stunts across the back yard. Finally, the twins returned to whatever secret mission they had going on behind the garage.

Grandma turned to Becca and asked, "What was going on in the kitchen Tuesday night? Did you have company?"

"We were having a Bible study and, yes, we had company. His name is Mike Gibbons. He goes to church where we do," replied Becca.

"Were you studying to teach him the way to become a Christian?" suggested Grandma.

"No, Mike is already a Christian. We were studying Matthew 24," said Becca.

"Oh, yes, Matthew 24 – that is a challenging one," said Grandma with emphasis on 'challenging'. "What did you learn?" she continued as she spread the lap robe across her knees.

"I learned that Matthew 24 is 'a challenging one'," laughed Becca, but then she continued more seriously. "What do you know about Matthew 24?"

"Well, I know that it has caused lots of controversy over the years," said Grandma, looking straight at Becca. Becca had never seen such focus in her grandma's eyes before. It was as if something had awakened there – an intelligence and depth that Grandma had not called upon for some time.

Grandma continued in an amused voice, "What's wrong, Becca? You look surprised that I know something about Matthew 24. I'm old, but I haven't lost my mind yet."

"I'm sorry, Grandma. You're right. I should have realized that you would know the answer," apologized Becca.

"Well, I didn't say I know the answer," said Grandma with a smile. "Your grandpa and I had quite a few Bible studies ourselves." And then more seriously, Grandma added in a quiet voice, "I know your grandpa was never quite sure."

"Yeah, I know. Which part is the Destruction of Jerusalem and which part is the Second Coming?" said Becca in agreement.

"No, that's not the hardest part," continued Grandma. Becca looked at Grandma. Grandma was staring off into space or perhaps she was looking into the past. Becca waited. Finally, Grandma turned to Becca and quoted, *"Verily I say unto you, this generation shall not pass, till all these things be fulfilled."*

Becca felt her stomach turn over. It was as if Grandma had read her mind. "Yeah, that's the question, all right," said Becca softly.

Grandma took a sip of tea and, while looking off across the yard, inquired, "What got this study started in the first place?"

Becca replied softly, "I realized I didn't know what happens to a person when he dies. If he is waiting for the Resurrection at the Second Coming of Christ, where is he? Is he in the grave?"

"Well, yes, I can see we have quite a bit of studying ahead of us," said Grandma gently, but also matter-of-factly.

Becca realized that Grandma was saying *we* and *us*, so she added, "Dad and I agreed to study on Tuesday night and Mike asked to come, and then Mom joined us, too. We compared Matthew 24 and Luke 17, but that just caused more questions." Becca paused. "For next week, Dad suggested we study Luke 21 and I Thessalonians, uh something, I forget which chapter."

"Probably chapter four," filled in Grandma. "It's about the Second Coming."

Becca smiled. Her grandma was truly amazing. "Yeah, that's it."

Her grandma began to stir, "Help me up, Becca, it's getting a bit too cool out here."

As Becca helped her grandma into the house, she yelled back over her shoulder, "Joe! Jim! Come in! Homework time!"

After helping Grandma into her room, Becca stepped back to the porch just in time to catch Joe and Jim scarfing down the cookies that Becca and Grandma had left. "Hey, you've already had your snack," scolded Becca even though she didn't really care. Both boys gave her the ugly face, which she returned and they all went into the house.

The boys worked on their homework while Becca looked at the notes Mom had left about supper: chicken breasts marinating in the refrigerator, mashed potatoes, salad, and, for dessert, pound cake with jam. Mom always planned a great dinner for Thursday night, even though Becca had to prepare it. Come to think of it, she probably arranged that because Becca had to prepare it and because it gave Dad an opportunity to brag on her.

At the dinner table that night, Grandma turned to her son, saying, "Well, Frank, I hear you're having a Bible study about Matthew 24."

Becca's dad looked quickly at his mother, then at Becca. "Yeah, I mean, yes, we are. Becca and I had some questions, so we decided we would study together." Dad gave Becca a quick smile and a wink.

"Well, what you have started on is no small study. It will end up being connected to almost every topic in the Bible," said Grandma.

"Really?" said Dad with a little laugh, then more seriously, "Really?"

"So, if it's all right with you, Son, and with you, Becca, I think I had better join you in this study," said Grandma. Becca's mom smiled: she was confident that Grandma would agree with her.

"Sure, that would be great," returned Dad, "but, I'm pretty sure I know what your position will be," said Dad who had caught the smile on Beth's face.

"Well, I'm pretty sure you don't," replied Grandma. Becca smiled, but the smiles on both Mom's and Dad's faces changed to expressions of surprise.

Her dad continued, "Dad always preached that the Second Coming was in the future."

"Of course, it's future," interjected Becca's mom. "The world is still standing, isn't it?"

Grandma looked at Beth and then back to Frank and then, in a voice of parental authority, stated, "I know what your dad preached, but I also know what your dad wasn't sure about." For a moment Grandma held Frank's eyes with hers before she dropped her eyes to her dinner plate. Then, in a clear voice of self assertion, Grandma continued, "Anyway, can't I have an opinion of my own?"

There was silence around the table for a few moments. Mom and Becca cleared away the dinner plates and got the dessert. Her dad had been looking thoughtfully at his mother. Like Becca, he now appreciated that his mom, though old in years, still possessed a clear intellect and a fire within. He smiled and said, "I look forward to studying with you, Mother. I look forward to it very much." Then he added, "We're studying Matthew 24, Luke 17, Luke 21 and I Thessalonians 4."

Grandma added, "And you need to include Matthew 5:17-18." She looked at Frank and, assuming he didn't know the passage, she quoted,

"Think not that I am come to destroy the Law, or the Prophets: I am not come to destroy, but to fulfill. For verily I say unto you, till heaven and earth pass, one jot or one tittle shall in no wise pass from the law, till all be fulfilled."

The twins had not followed much of the table conversation, but they recognized that Grandma was quoting scripture. They looked around the table as everyone stared at Grandma. They put down their forks and looked at one another. Each wondered, 'Was it all right to eat? Was there going to be a prayer?'

Finally, Dad spoke, "Well, we know the Old Law passed away at the cross." Mom nodded in happy agreement with Dad.

"Was everything fulfilled at the cross?" Grandma asked, emphasizing 'everything'.

Becca's dad repeated the question as if to make sure he understood it. "Was *everything* fulfilled at the cross?" He did not know how to answer that question.

Grandma concluded, "We have a lot to study." Turning to Becca she added, "I'm looking forward to meeting Mr. Mike Gibbons. Frank, I'm feeling a little dizzy. Would you help me back to my bed now?"

As Frank helped his mom to her room, he asked, "Mom, are you not feeling well?"

His mom replied, "I've just been feeling really tired lately and sometimes I get dizzy. I'm just not as spry as I used to be."

That night before Becca went to bed, she read Matthew 5:17-18. When her grandma had quoted it at supper, Becca had not understood exactly how it tied into the Destruction of Jerusalem or the Second Coming, but as she read and reread it now, she began to see the connection. She knew about the Old Law that the Israelites lived under and how Christ had brought the New Law or New Covenant, the Gospel. So Matthew 5:17-18 was saying that the Old Law would not pass out of existence or force until all was fulfilled. Becca realized the importance of the word *all*, the same word that was troubling her in Matthew 24:34: *'all these things'*, *'in that generation'*. Now, here was this scripture saying '... *till heaven and earth pass, one jot or one tittle shall in no wise pass from the law, till __all__ be fulfilled'*. Becca stepped to her window. The neighborhood below looked calm and serene and

54

the stars in their silent beauty were starting to appear in the sky above, but Becca did not feel calm or serene in her heart. She had too many questions. She had the feeling that this study, this search for the truth, was going to be a life-changing journey.

Her grandma had certainly surprised everyone today. Grandma had her own opinion and it did not sound as if she had always agreed with George Alexander Elliott. Furthermore, Grandma had said that even George Alexander Elliott wasn't sure about what he had preached. Becca had always thought of her grandpa as the hero, the gospel preacher who had led many – maybe even hundreds – to faith and salvation in Christ. Suddenly, she was having to deal with the knowledge that, even though that was true, her grandpa had sometimes been unsure and troubled by scriptures that did not fit the truth as he had understood it. There had been scriptures that he did not understand. He and Grandma had studied together and had possibly come to different conclusions.

Becca looked up into the night sky and uttered this prayer, "Heavenly Father, help us as we study to know and understand your truth." This prayer was also on the lips of her mom and dad in the bedroom below, in the thoughts of Mike across town, and in the heart of Grandma in the magical room below.

Chapter 8
Heaven and Earth

Sunday dawned a beautiful fall morning. There was a crisp chill in the air that foretold of colder days to come, but today there was sunshine and the trees along the drive to the church building showed their colors of crimson and gold. The car was full this morning. Joe was in the front between Mom and Dad, while Jim hunkered in the back between Becca and Grandma. Neither boy was happy about the seating arrangements, but of the two, Joe had less to grumble about. At least, he was sitting in the front seat. They left for church a little earlier than usual in order to get a parking place on the side of the building that would allow Grandma to enter on the ground level and avoid the front steps.

Becca assisted Grandma out of the car and into the building. "Which class do you want to go to, Grandma? The auditorium class or the preacher's class with Mom and Dad," suggested Becca.

Grandma turned and motioned to her son. Frank stepped closer to hear her. "Frank, did you say that the new preacher was the one who was teaching on Matthew 24?"

"No, Mom. Becca's class is studying Matthew 24, but I think you will be interested in the class Beth and I attend. Our class is taught by Brother Owens, the new preacher, and he is really challenging us with some teachings that aren't exactly traditional," said Frank.

"I'll go to class with you then," said Grandma, taking Frank's arm. Mrs. Gardner had noticed Grandma and was coming their way, so Becca left Grandma in Dad's care and turned down the hall toward her class. Becca liked Mrs. Gardner but knew that once Mrs. Gardner started talking, she talked on and on, making it hard to get away.

Since there were still several minutes before class time, no one was in Becca's classroom. She checked the college classroom, seeing only a couple girls whom she didn't know. She decided to go out to the front steps of the building, hoping she would meet Mike as he arrived. Brother Owens was also on the front steps, greeting people. Becca said, "Good morning," then moved over to the side out of the way, but Brother Owens followed her.

"I believe your name is Becca, Becca Elliott," volunteered Brother Owens.

"Yes, sir," returned Becca.

"It certainly is a beautiful morning, isn't it?" continued Brother Owens.

"Yes, it is," affirmed Becca. Brother Owens turned to greet a family who was coming up the steps. Looking toward the parking lot, Becca saw Mike getting out of his car. Becca wondered why Mike had not ridden to church with his parents. She knew he was living at home to avoid the housing costs at the college.

Taking two steps at a time, Mike hurried up to Becca and said, "Hey there."

"Hi," said Becca, smiling at Mike and using her hand to shade her eyes from the morning sun.

"Are you out here waiting for anyone special?" asked Mike with a little bit of a tease.

Becca smiled and said, "Yeah, I'm waiting for Ben."

"Oh, OK then. Excuse me," said Mike in a serious voice, but then he couldn't keep the grin off his face. "Well, shall we continue to wait or can we go on in?" asked Mike.

"Let's go in," agreed Becca smiling. As they made their way down the hall, Becca asked Mike, "What are you studying in your class?"

"Uh…. we're studying in the book of Acts, I think, yeah, Acts," answered Mike.

"Well, if you hear anything that will help our study, jot it down," encouraged Becca.

"You bet I will. Have you read the passage your dad suggested in Thessalonians?" asked Mike. "It surely sounds like the Second Coming of Christ would be hard to miss: people coming out the ground and rising up to meet Christ in the air. I think some churches call it the *Rapture*. I don't see how that could have happened in that generation without there having been some record. And if Christ took the saved to heaven then, how are we going to get there? Is He coming back again?" Becca could hear the frustration in his voice. Mike looked at Becca with a questioning expression on his face. Becca shrugged her shoulders with an 'I-don't-know' expression on her face.

"Sorry about that. I didn't mean to get so intense," apologized Mike.

"It's OK. I have questions, too. In fact, I'm going to ask Mr. Simms a couple of them this morning. Remember, my class is studying Matthew 24," said Becca.

"Oh, yeah," said Mike. Leaning a little closer to Becca, he asked, "Will you wait for me here after class?" Becca nodded as Mike entered his classroom and Becca went on to hers, trying hard not to smile so big that she would attract attention.

Mr. Simms was beginning class, so Becca quickly took a seat, noticing that Jenny wasn't there. Becca decided to phone her this afternoon to check on her. Jenny was always at services – her family was very faithful in attendance. Her father was one of the leaders of the congregation.

Mr. Simms began with a question, "Did anyone read the rest of Matthew 24?" Becca raised her hand; however, she was the only who did. "In that case, we will read it together. Becca, would you begin in verse 29?" asked Mr. Simms.

Becca began, anticipating that after a few verses, Mr. Simms would stop her and choose another student to read. However, Becca had read these verses so many times during the past week that she was now able to read them with expression and emphasis that helped the reading to be more easily understood. Mr. Simms did not ask Becca to stop until she had finished the chapter. "Thank you, Becca. That was excellent." Several students were staring at Becca, wondering if she was trying to show off, while others were obviously impressed.

Mr. Simms asked the class a question, hoping a rash of guessing wouldn't break out this morning, "Can someone tell us what these verses are describing?" When several students raised their hands, Mr. Simms called on one. "This is the Second Coming of Christ," the student answered.

"Very good," replied Mr. Simms encouraged. "And what are some of the main themes that are in this reading?" he continued.

The question about 'themes' was harder, so there were no volunteers. Mr. Simms rephrased the question, "What about the Second Coming? When will it be?"

Hands went up again. "No one knows."

"If we don't know when it will be, what should we do?" asked Mr. Simms. Finally, there was a volunteer, "Live right and always be ready."

"Yes, that's right. Can you tell me which verse says that?" asked Mr. Simms.

Several students were racing to see who could answer first and soon two students both volunteered, "Verse 44."

Mr. Simms was very encouraged with the class participation today and continued to quiz them, having them search for verses and read them aloud. Becca began to worry that she was not going to have an opportunity to ask Mr. Simms about verse 34, but, finally, during a pause while Mr. Simms thought about what to ask next, Becca interjected, "Mr. Simms?"

"Yes, Becca," replied Mr. Simms.

"I have a question about verse 34," began Becca.

"Will you read the verse out loud for the class, please?" asked Mr. Simms.

Becca said, "I'll start with verse 32:

'Now learn a parable of the fig tree; when his branch is yet tender, and putteth forth leaves, ye know that it is near, even at the doors. So likewise ye, when ye shall see all these things, know that it is near, even at the doors. Verily I say unto you, this generation shall not pass, till all these things be fulfilled.'"

Becca looked up at Mr. Simms, who seemed to be silently rereading the verses.

The only sound for several moments was from a couple of boys on the back row who had been playing tic-tac-toe. When the classroom fell silent, they too looked up to see what was going on.

Finally, Mr. Simms said, "And what is your question, Becca?"

Becca explained, "Well, Jesus is the one talking. He has talked about tribulation, the Destruction of Jerusalem, and His Second Coming, and then He says that all these things will happen in that generation. How could that be?"

"Well, certainly the tribulation and the Destruction of Jerusalem did happen in that generation, but He said that no one knew the day or the hour when the Second Coming would be," explained Mr. Simms.

Becca continued, "Well, verse 29 bothers me, too. If He had been talking about the tribulation that would happen in that generation, verse 29 says,

'Immediately after the tribulation of those days shall the sun be darkened, and the moon shall not give her light, and the stars shall fall from heaven, and the powers of the heavens shall be shaken...'

and He goes on to talk about the Second Coming, and well, my point is, that it sounds as if the Second Coming was to be immediately after the tribulation. If the tribulation happened in that generation, then the Second Coming must have happened immediately after." Becca looked up at Mr. Simms, but Mr. Simms continued to stare at his Bible. Becca continued, "And another question, Mr. Simms. I was reading a book on the Olivet Discourse that my dad got from our church library. The author of the book said that, clearly, Jesus said that He would return in that generation but that He didn't."

"Well, Becca," began Mr. Simms, "we know that the Second Coming hasn't happened yet, so maybe we are not understanding what Christ meant when He made this statement or perhaps there's a mistranslation." Mr. Simms checked his watch before saying, "Oh, it's time for the bell. For next week, please read Matthew 25?" Mr. Simms turned, opened the door and allowed the students to leave before the dismissal bell rang.

Becca smiled apologetically at Mr. Simms as she passed out of the room. She now realized that she had put him on the spot. She had assumed that the adults knew the answers, but she was learning that, evidently, that is not always the case. She had to wait only a minute for the bell and for Mike to join her in the hall.

Neither of them spoke but started down the hall side by side. Mike took hold of Becca's arm right above the elbow as he guided and followed her through the people outside the auditorium. They sat on a pew a couple of rows behind the other young people. He whispered to her, "Did you get to ask your question?"

"Yes, but I didn't get any answers, other than we must not understand what Jesus meant when He said He would return in that generation," whispered Becca.

"Mr. Simms is right about that. I don't understand," added Mike.

The song leader asked the congregation to stand as they sang, "*We praise thee, O God...*"

Today's sermon did not have any new ideas that Becca had not heard before. It was on one of her favorite topics, the grace of God. Even when God knew how terrible man would be, He still gave His Son to die so that, if a person would believe that Jesus was the Son of God and obey God's will, then all that person's sins - no matter how bad - would be forgiven and forgotten.

* * *

No one talked much on the way home from church, but the conversation at lunch centered on the Sunday school classes.

"Becca, how did your study of Matthew 24 go this morning?" asked Dad.

"OK, I guess," Becca said with a shrug. "I asked Mr. Simms about verse 34 and he said we must not understand what Christ meant when He said that He would return in that generation."

Becca's mom started to say something, but Dad jumped in first, "We had an interesting study this morning in Isaiah. What did you think about it, Mom?" Becca's dad directed the question to his mother.

"I think everything that young preacher said was right. It was a good lesson," said Grandma. "There are a lot of good prophecies in Isaiah about the Messiah and the New Heavens and the New Earth."

Becca heard what Grandma said and, as she considered it for a moment, she realized that this was new to her. She had not heard of a New Heavens or a New Earth. She asked, "New Heavens and New Earth? What New Heavens and New Earth? I thought the earth would be destroyed at the Second Coming? I thought we went to Heaven, you know, the Heaven that already is, you know, where God is. I never heard of a *New* Heaven and *New* Earth." Becca felt very confused and frustrated.

Grandma knew Becca was frustrated but she wanted to put one more thought into her mind, so Grandma continued, "Remember the verse I quoted at dinner the other night?"

"Yeah, I mean, yes," Becca corrected herself.

"What did it say about Heaven and earth?" prodded Grandma.

Becca did not answer immediately: she couldn't remember exactly what it said. Finally, she tried, "It was about the Old Law passing away."

Grandma quoted again,

"'Think not that I am come to destroy the law, or the prophets: I am not come to destroy, but to fulfill. For verily I say unto you, till <u>heaven and earth</u> pass, one jot or one tittle shall in no wise pass from the law, till all be fulfilled.'

It sounds to me like the passing away of Heaven and earth would allow the Old Law to pass away – maybe to make way for a New Heaven and New Earth," Grandma paused, then added, "The New Heaven and New Earth of the Messiah."

Becca and her dad were both carefully considering what Grandma had just said.

Mom, however, was quick to speak, "But Heaven and Earth did not pass away; they are still here."

In a moment, Dad added more slowly, not sure that what he was about to say was right or not, but it certainly seemed connected, "What passed away was the Old Covenant and it was replaced by the New Covenant. Do you mean to say that the Old Covenant was the Old

Heavens and Old Earth and the New Covenant is the New Heavens and New Earth?"

"Exactly right," said Grandma matter-of-factly.

Becca's mom shook her head and exhaled in a way that said she didn't agree as she began clearing the dishes away. Becca ran to get a paper and pencil and returned to Grandma. "Where is that scripture you quoted in Matthew?"

"Matthew 5:17-18," said Grandma.

"Oh, yeah, I already have that one. Where in Isaiah is the prophecy of the New Heaven and New Earth?" asked Becca.

"Isaiah 65:17," said Grandma.

"Thanks," said Becca as she disappeared upstairs. As soon as she got upstairs, she remembered the dinner dishes and kitchen that had to be cleaned up. She threw her note on the bed and hurried back down to the kitchen to help Mom.

While she and Mom were loading the dishwasher, Becca's mom paused for a moment and said, "Becca, you are doing a good thing by studying the Bible and exploring passages that you may not be familiar with, but I also want you to remember not to reject teachings that have stood the test of time."

Becca thought about what her mother had said, but several exceptions occurred to her that made her think that perhaps *time* was not the test of *truth*. For thousands of years man believed that the earth was flat. When Galileo tried to show the people of his day that neither was the earth flat nor did the sun revolve around the earth, but rather the earth revolved around the sun, he was branded as a heretic. Many religious institutions have existed for hundreds of years and yet disagree vehemently with each other. No, Becca did not think that *time* was a test for *truth*.

Chapter 9
Isaiah 65

Later that afternoon, Becca read Isaiah 65:17 and several verses following it. Then, hoping to understand better, she dropped back to the first verse and read the entire chapter. She thought she understood some verses but was unsure of others. She marked her place, taking her Bible as she went downstairs to find Grandma.

Grandma was sitting in her room, her Bible resting on her lap as if she was expecting Becca; but her head was laid back and her eyes were closed.

"Grandma, may I come in?" asked Becca.

"Of course, Dear," answered Grandma.

When Becca saw the Bible, she asked, "Have you been reading the Bible, too?"

"I tried to do some reading, but I became dizzy and my eyes blurred. I wanted to read Isaiah 65."

"Me, too," said Becca. "But I do not understand what I'm reading."

"Okay," said Grandma. "If you will do the reading, we can discuss it together."

Isa 65:1 "I was sought by those who did not ask for Me;
I was found by those who did not seek Me.

I said, 'Here I am, here I am,'
To a nation that was not called by My name.

After reading verse one, Becca suggested, "It sounds as if some people who did not know God, or even look for God, found him anyway, and He welcomed them."

"Very good, you're exactly right. Do you know who those people are?" inquired Grandma.

"No, I don't," answered Becca.

"Well then, let's remember that question. Maybe in our studies we will find out who those people were. Try verses 2-5," encouraged Grandma.

Isaiah 65: 2 I have stretched out My hands
all day long to a rebellious people,
Who walk in a way that is not good,
According to their own thoughts;
3 A people who provoke Me to anger continually to My face;
Who sacrifice in gardens,
And burn incense on altars of brick;
4 Who sit among the graves,
And spend the night in the tombs;
Who eat swine's flesh,
And the broth of abominable things is in their vessels;
5 Who say, 'Keep to yourself,
Do not come near me,
For I am holier than you!'
These are smoke in My nostrils,
A fire that burns all the day.

After Becca read the verses through twice, she ventured, "It sounds like there was a people whom God did welcome and wanted to help, but they chose to be evil instead. They did not answer God's invitation."

"Becca, your dad is right; you are a very intelligent girl. I believe you understand more than you give yourself credit for. Try verses 6-7."

> *Isa 65:6 "Behold, it is written before Me:*
> *I will not keep silence, but will repay —*
> *Even repay into their bosom —*
> *7 Your iniquities and the iniquities of your fathers together,"*
> *Says the LORD,*
> *"Who have burned incense on the mountains*
> *And blasphemed Me on the hills;*
> *Therefore I will measure their former work into their bosom."*

"I think," said Becca, "that God is going to punish them for their wickedness. That's what he means by *repay*; it's like paybacks or getting even with someone."

"Well, I guess so. They are going to receive what they deserve. You are doing just fine. Verses 8-10."

> *Isa 65:8 Thus says the LORD:*
> *"As the new wine is found in the cluster,*
> *And one says, 'Do not destroy it,*
> *For a blessing is in it,'*
> *So will I do for My servants' sake,*
> *That I may not destroy them all.*
> *9 I will bring forth descendants from Jacob,*
> *And from Judah an heir of My mountains;*
> *My elect shall inherit it,*
> *And My servants shall dwell there.*
> *10 Sharon shall be a fold of flocks,*

And the Valley of Achor a place for herds to lie down,
For My people who have sought Me.

"I don't understand the part about the new wine in the cluster, but then it sounds as if not everyone is going to be destroyed. So, I guess the punishment from verses 6 & 7 is destruction, but not everyone will be destroyed. Some will inherit, uh …I'm not sure what they will inherit. It says 'my elect'. I've heard some preachers call the church the elect of God. Is that right?" asked Becca.

"Well, that may be true, but let's not conclude that just yet – or just because we heard someone say that. Remember, we are taking a *fresh* look at the scriptures and we don't want to be influenced by what we have heard in the past. Let's keep an open mind. Try verses 11-16," encouraged Grandma.

Before looking at the next verse Becca said, "Except for that comment about the elect, I am not being influenced by anything, because I have never studied these scriptures." Becca continued to read:

Isa 65:11 "But you are those who forsake the LORD,
Who forget My holy mountain,
Who prepare a table for Gad,
And who furnish a drink offering for Meni.
12 Therefore I will number you for the sword, And you shall all bow down to the slaughter; Because, when I called, you did not answer; When I spoke, you did not hear, But did evil before My eyes, And chose that in which I do not delight."
13 Therefore thus says the Lord GOD:
"Behold, My servants shall eat,
But you shall be hungry;
Behold, My servants shall drink,
But you shall be thirsty;
Behold, My servants shall rejoice,

But you shall be ashamed;
14 Behold, My servants shall sing for joy of heart,
But you shall cry for sorrow of heart, And wail for grief of spirit.
15 You shall leave your name as a curse to My chosen; For the
Lord GOD will slay you, And call His servants by another name;
16 So that he who blesses himself in the earth Shall bless himself
in the God of truth; And he who swears in the earth Shall swear
by the God of truth; Because the former troubles are forgotten,
And because they are hidden from My eyes.

Becca read the verses, thought a moment and said, "Now he's talking about the wicked, those who rejected him. He invited them but they would not come, so they are going to be hungry and thirsty. Those who answered God's invitation will eat, drink, and rejoice. He will slay the wicked and call His people another name. And the end of verse 16 says 'former troubles are forgotten".

"You are doing great! Go on to verses 17-19."

Isa 65:17"For behold, I create new heavens and a new earth;
And the former shall not be remembered or come to mind.
18 But be glad and rejoice forever in what I create;
For behold, I create Jerusalem as a rejoicing,
And her people a joy.
19 I will rejoice in Jerusalem,
And joy in My people;
The voice of weeping shall no longer be heard in her,
Nor the voice of crying.

After reading, Becca said, "Oh, this is where He makes the New Heavens and New Earth."

Grandma asked, "Who do you think the New Heaven and New Earth are for?"

Becca thought, smiled, and answered, "For those who answered the invitation." Becca looked at the verses again and said, "Verse nineteen says *'no weeping'*, as it's going to be in heaven."

"There you go again, repeating teaching you have already heard. You told me correctly what these verses meant the first time. There is no weeping in the New Heavens and New Earth that are prepared for those who answer the invitation. Let's not conclude yet about where or even when these New Heavens and New Earth are. Go on to verses 20-23."

> *Isa 65:20 "No more shall an infant from there live but a few days,*
> *Nor an old man who has not fulfilled his days;*
> *For the child shall die one hundred years old,*
> *But the sinner being one hundred years old shall be accursed.*
> *21 They shall build houses and inhabit them;*
> *They shall plant vineyards and eat their fruit.*
> *22 They shall not build and another inhabit;*
> *They shall not plant and another eat;*
> *For as the days of a tree, so shall be the days of My people,*
> *And My elect shall long enjoy the work of their hands.*
> *23 They shall not labor in vain,*
> *Nor bring forth children for trouble;*
> *For they shall be the descendants of the blessed of the LORD,*
> *And their offspring with them.*

Becca concluded that these verses promised that the people of God would prosper.

Grandma said, "And verses 24-25."

> *Isa 65:24 "It shall come to pass*
> *That before they call, I will answer;*
> *And while they are still speaking, I will hear.*
> *25 The wolf and the lamb shall feed together,*

The lion shall eat straw like the ox,
And dust shall be the serpent's food.
They shall not hurt nor destroy in all My holy mountain,"
Says the LORD.

Becca said, "It's a time of peace."

With a smile on her face, Grandma asked, "Do you think the wolf and the lamb will feed together?"

Becca paused only for a moment before she answered, "No, not literally. I took it as figurative language. It's a time of peace."

Grandma continued, "So, do you think that the *Heaven and Earth* are literal or figurative? Does the writer mean that there will physically be a New Heaven and a New Earth?"

"I don't know, Grandma. This is new to me. As I said earlier, I assumed that the saved went to Heaven and that the earth was destroyed. Anyway, how could a Heaven and earth be figurative?"

"Remember what your dad suggested at dinner. Figuratively, the Old Covenant is the Old Heavens and Earth, whereas the New Covenant is the New Heavens and New Earth. The Old Covenant controlled everything about their lives. When it was gone, their whole world and existence changed. Do you remember how we say that the world was *destroyed* by a flood in Noah's time?

Becca nodded in agreement.

"Think about it carefully. The world, the planet, the rocks, the mountains were not destroyed. It was the people who were destroyed. When Messiah came, it was the Heaven and Earth of the Old Covenant that was destroyed. The Destruction of the Temple and of the city of Jerusalem was a clear sign that the Heaven and Earth of the Old Covenant were destroyed." Grandma paused, then asked, "What do you think verse twenty-four means when it says, '*before they call, I will answer*'?

"I don't know," said Becca, shrugging her shoulders.

"Well, let me suggest a possible answer," said Grandma. "Christ came to earth to die for the sins of *all* people, not just for the Israelites, but for everyone – even for those who were not God's chosen people and didn't realize they needed God's forgiveness. He died for all future peoples who were not even born yet. Christ provided the answer before mankind knew a problem existed. Christ answered before we called." Grandma paused, then stated, "That's enough for today. I think I will lie down for a while."

After helping Grandma to her bed, Becca kissed Grandma on the cheek and softly closed the door on her way out. She went to the hall to make a phone call.

"Hello," answered the voice on the phone.

"Hi, Jenny. This is Becca. I missed you this morning. Are you sick?" Becca slid down the wall to rest on the floor. She and Jenny loved to talk on the phone and, unless Mom or Dad objected, this call would likely last a while.

"No, I'm fine. We went to church in Cedarvale this morning," replied Jenny.

"May I ask why? Do you know some people there?" asked Becca.

"My dad does and he wanted to talk to them about something."

"Did you get that English assignment finished? I still have to work on mine."

"Yeah, me, too. I have to go now. Good-bye." Jenny hung up on the other end. Becca was pretty sure something was going on with Jenny: she didn't want to come to the Bible study, she hadn't called in days, and she was acting as if she didn't even want to talk to Becca. Becca wondered what was wrong.

While she was still sitting in the hall floor, the phone rang. Becca answered, "Hello, Elliott's residence."

"Hello, this is Mike Gibbons, may I talk to Becca?"

"Hi, Mike. It's me."

"Hi, what are you doing?"

"Nothing much," replied Becca.

"Nothing much?" teased Mike.

"Well, actually, Grandma and I were reading Isaiah 65. It is sort of hard, but you should read it. It's about a people who rejected God's invitation and a people who accepted, as well as about a New Heaven and New Earth."

"Isaiah 65? OK. I'll have to read it if I want to keep up with you. I called to make sure our study is still on for Tuesday night?"

"Yeah, Tuesday night at seven o'clock," answered Becca. "Oh, Mike, do you mind if I ask you a personal question?" asked Becca.

"Go ahead. Ask away," replied Mike.

"Well, I noticed you drove your own car to church this morning and I wondered why you didn't come with your parents. Aren't you still living at home?" Becca regretted asking as soon as the question was out of her mouth. "Oh, I'm sorry. I shouldn't have asked. It's none of my business," said Becca.

"Hey, it's no big deal. Sometimes I drive my car if I have somewhere different to go after church and sometimes I ride with my parents, especially if I know Mom is making my favorite foods for lunch. But, today, I drove my car because my parents decided to visit at Cedarvale and I didn't want to go with them. Actually, I wanted to see you," added Mike.

Becca was glad they were talking on the phone because she felt herself blush. He did like her. "Thanks, that's nice of you to say. I was glad to see you, too." Then she thought about Jenny and added, "What a coincidence! Jenny's family went to Cedarvale this morning, too."

"Well, I'm not sure it's a coincidence, but I don't want to make any speculations about it."

Becca wanted to ask more, but she decided she had already been forward enough so she restrained herself.

Mike said, "I will see you Tuesday night then."

After they said goodbye, Becca went upstairs to finish her English assignment. She stood at her window for a few minutes, thinking about Mike. Instead of going with his parents, he had chosen to see her. He had even wanted to sit with her during worship. Becca smiled as she turned to begin her homework.

Chapter 10
Tuesday Night Number Two

1 Thess 4:13   But I do not want you to be ignorant, brethren, concerning those who have fallen asleep, lest you sorrow as others who have no hope. 14 For if we believe that Jesus died and rose again, even so God will bring with Him those who sleep in Jesus.

15 For this we say to you by the word of the Lord, that we who are alive and remain until the coming of the Lord will by no means precede those who are asleep. 16 For the Lord Himself will descend from heaven with a shout, with the voice of an archangel, and with the trumpet of God. And the dead in Christ will rise first. 17 Then we who are alive and remain shall be caught up together with them in the clouds to meet the Lord in the air. And thus we shall always be with the Lord. 18 Therefore comfort one another with these words.

5:1 But concerning the times and the seasons, brethren, you have no need that I should write to you. 2 For you yourselves know perfectly that the day of the Lord so comes as a thief in the night. 3 For when they say, "Peace and safety!" then sudden destruction comes upon them, as labor pains upon a pregnant woman. And they shall not escape. 4 But you, brethren, are not in darkness, so that this Day should overtake you as a thief. 5 You are all sons of light and sons of the day. We are not of the night nor of darkness. 6 Therefore let us not sleep, as others do, but let us watch and be sober. 7 For those who sleep, sleep at night, and those who get drunk are drunk at night. 8 But let us who are of the day be sober, putting on the breastplate of faith and love, and as a helmet the hope of salvation. 9 For God did not appoint us to wrath, but to obtain salvation through our Lord Jesus Christ, 10 who died for us, that whether we wake or sleep, we should live together with Him.

11 Therefore comfort each other and edify one another, just as you also are doing.

On Tuesday night the number at the study table increased by one with Grandma sitting next to Becca. The twins were once again restricted to their room. After Becca introduced Mike to Grandma, everyone turned to Dad to take the lead.

Dad began, "I asked everyone last week to read Luke 21 and I Thessalonians 4:13 through 5:11. Plus, I think some people have also been looking at Isaiah 65 this week. So does anyone want to start us off tonight?" When no one volunteered, Dad continued, "Well, then, let's start with Luke 21. Does everyone see that Luke and Matthew are parallel passages, but that the events are not recorded in the same order?

Becca placed the poster which they had made the previous Tuesday night on the table for all to see. She began, "I thought it was interesting how the apostles asked about when the Destruction of the Temple would be and what would be the signs that it was about to happen. Jesus answered their question but also went on to talk about the Second Coming. And the way He spoke about His Second Coming made it sound as if it would happen in the same generation as the Destruction of the Temple. Verse twenty-seven says, *'He will come in the clouds'* and verse thirty-two states, '*this generation will by no means pass away till all things take place*'."

Mike interrupted, "I don't see how that could be. If Christ came in the clouds with the archangel and with trumpets, then surely there would be some writing or testimony that it happened. And if the earth was supposed to be burned up with fire at the Second Coming, how can we still be here on the earth?"

Grandma gestured with her hand as if to say 'calm down'. When all had turned to look at her, she smiled, "If I may make a suggestion…" She paused and they all indicated that they wanted to hear her idea. "I think you may have started in the wrong place. If you start in the New Testament without looking at the background of the Old Testament, you will easily be confused and perhaps come to some wrong conclusions. Let's look at Matt 5:17-18, again."

They all turned to Matthew 5.

Matt 5:17 "Do not think that I came to destroy the Law or the Prophets. I did not come to destroy but to fulfill. 18 For assuredly, I say to you, till heaven and earth pass away, one jot or one tittle will by no means pass from the law till all is fulfilled.

Grandma continued, "Notice that Jesus said that He came to fulfill the Law and the Prophets. Therefore, Jesus must do everything that the Law and the Prophets promised He would do. And when it is all fulfilled, the Old Law, the First Covenant that was made with Israel, will pass away. Look again at Luke 21 verse 22." Grandma waited while they found the passage.

Luke 21:22 For these are the days of vengeance, that all things which are written may be fulfilled.

"Here Christ says, *'these are the days of vengeance, that all things which are written may be fulfilled'*. I believe when Christ said 'these days' He really meant the days in which that generation of people were living. Jesus' ministry was in 30-33 A.D. and the destruction of Jerusalem was in 70 A.D., a period of about 40 years. Some of the people to whom he was speaking could very well have been alive to see the Destruction of the Temple. Look at Luke 9:27." All had been listening carefully to what Grandma was saying and immediately turned to the scripture.

"Would you read it to us, Mike?" Grandma asked.

Mike read,

"But I tell you truly, there are some standing here who shall not taste death till they see the kingdom of God."

"Becca, will you read Matthew 16:28?" requested Grandma.

Becca turned to that passage and read,

"Assuredly, I say to you, there are some standing here who shall not taste death till they see the Son Man coming in His kingdom."

"Oh, excuse me, I got off the point I wanted to make," said Grandma. "I wanted to emphasize a point about the Law and the Prophets. Here is my point: Everything Jesus did was to fulfill the Law and the Prophets. If we want to understand the things that Jesus did and said, it would help to know what the Law and the Prophets had recorded concerning Him. Even the apostle Paul wrote that the gospel which he preached was from the Law and the Prophets. Frank, would you read Acts 28:23?" Grandma continued while Dad was locating the passage, "Now what Frank is going to read is about the apostle Paul and how he taught people about Jesus."

Frank turned in his Bible and read,

"So when they had appointed him a day, many came to him at his lodging, to whom he explained and solemnly testified of the kingdom of God, persuading them concerning Jesus from both the Law of Moses and the Prophets, from morning till evening."

"So, I say again – and I think this is very important – if we want to understand what Jesus said and did, then we need to know what the Law and the Prophets said about Him and about what He would do. When Becca and I were reading in Isaiah 65 the other day, she did a very good job explaining what it was saying. Becca, do you think you could summarize it for us?" asked Grandma.

Becca looked a little unsure but offered, "I'll try if you will help me." Becca thought for a moment and began, "There was a people whom God had invited to Him, but these people rejected His invitation, so they were going to be punished. Grandma said that they were going to get what they deserved." Becca smiled at Grandma. "But there was another group of people who did answer God's invitation and He promised to cause them to prosper. It sounded as if they were going to receive a New Heaven and a New Earth."

Becca's Dad spoke up, "Yes, that's what we have been studying with Brother Owens in our Sunday school class. The people whom God had chosen and called to be faithful to Him were the Children of Israel – the Israelites. But they were rarely faithful to God and were often involved in idolatrous worship. When God sent His Son, the Messiah, they rejected and crucified Him. But some Jews, like Peter, James, and John and the other disciples, did believe. On the day of Pentecost, three thousand believed and obeyed. Paul later preached the Gospel invitation to the Gentiles, who were not God's people, and many of them believed."

Becca interrupted, "The Gentiles! That must be the people who did not seek God but found Him anyway." Grandma was nodding her head in agreement with Becca.

Dad continued, "Those who believed in Christ, that He is the Son of God, are the people of the New Covenant."

Grandma interrupted this time, "Yes, but before we can have the New Covenant, the Old Covenant has to pass away; and, for the Old Covenant to pass away scripture states that *all* of it must be fulfilled." Grandma had emphasized *all*. "So, what we need to know is what was prophesied. According to Jesus' own words, if it had been prophesied, it would be fulfilled in *'that generation'*. That generation would see the coming of the New Covenant."

Mom spoke up this time, "Yes, I think that is right. The Old Covenant passed away and the New Covenant came in that generation; but, that does not mean Christ's Second Coming was in that generation. The Second Coming of Christ and the Resurrection are promises of the New Covenant."

Everyone looked at Becca's mom, considering what she said. Then Becca asked, "Was the Second Coming of Christ prophesized in the Old Testament?"

Dad added, "And the Resurrection and the Judgment? Are they prophesied in the Old Testament?"

Mom interjected again, "No, I think those are promises of the New Covenant."

"Do you know what I think would be a good idea?" asked Grandma as they all turned to her. "I think we should invite Brother Owens to our study group."

Dad nodded his head, "Yes, I had thought about that myself. If he can come, that will be good. I'll talk to him this week."

Since Mike had a concerned look on his face, Dad asked, "Mike, is something wrong?"

"Well, Mr. Elliott, there may be. Were you aware that three families were not at our congregation Sunday morning: my parents, Jenny's parents, and the Collins?" Mike hesitated. Everyone waited for him to continue. "They all went to church at the Cedarvale congregation to have a meeting with the leaders there." Mike took a deep breath. "They are concerned because they think that Brother Owens is teaching *heresy*. The issue all centers on the Second Coming of Christ: is it *past or future*?"

Dad was quickly growing red in the face, "Heresy! I have not heard any heresy. I have heard good teaching on scriptures that we have ignored for years. He has opened my mind to study the Bible. What's wrong with studying the Bible and considering new ideas? I want to know what the Bible teaches. I want to know the truth!"

Mom interjected, "I'm not sure that what Brother Owens is teaching about the Second Coming is right or not. I still believe the Second Coming is future, but I am willing to study it. But if he teaches that it is past when I conclude it is future, then I won't worship where he preaches. Either he will go or I will go."

Everyone looked at Becca's mom, then at each other, except Grandma who was looking at her Bible. Grandma spoke softly, "Beth, I know you are a staunch supporter of one Truth, and I admire that; but, for many years, Frank's father and I struggled with this very question. Even though George continued to preach the traditional view from the pulpit, he was unsure and once tried to talk to one of the church leaders about it. Since that man was a good student of the Bible, George hoped that they could study together; but he dismissed the idea as ridiculous and wouldn't even consider studying the passages that were causing concern for George and me. We continued to study together and, well, we came to different conclusions. He continued to preach the traditional view; but I believe that we have misunderstood the nature of the Second Coming. I look forward to studying with Brother Owens. I hope he can clear up some difficult points for me. I don't have all the answers. I need help to understand. I want to know what the Truth really is."

Dad repeated, "I'll invite Brother Owens to study with us. Beth, I understand your concerns and I appreciate the fact that you are willing to study with us. Mike, I hope you will continue to come, too."

After everyone said goodnight, Becca followed Mike to the front porch. Mike turned to Becca, "It's only 8:30; do you want to go get a Coke, I mean Dr. Pepper, at the drive-in?"

"Oh, I'm sorry. We didn't offer you anything to drink tonight."

"I'm glad you didn't. It gives me an opportunity to get some time alone with you," said Mike.

"Just a minute," said Becca with a smile that said 'I like you, too'. When Becca went back inside, Mom and Dad were talking in the kitchen. They stopped when she came in. "Mike and I are going to the drive-in. I'll be back soon."

Dad smiled and gave her a wave that said 'OK'.

Becca now found it very easy to talk to Mike. They talked about what classes Mike was taking at college, what he planned to major in, and what he wanted to do as a career. They talked about the high school football game and Mike speculated on their chances of winning. Since Mike had played football, he knew the coach and most of this year's team.

"Hey, how about I pick you up at 5:30 on Friday? We'll get something to eat and then go to the game," suggested Mike.

"That will be great," replied Becca with a smile. Mike had finally asked her on a real date.

As they were pulling up to Becca's house about 30 minutes later, the conversation turned back to the Bible study. Becca asked, "Mike, if your parents don't like what Brother Owens is teaching, won't they be upset that you are studying with him?"

"Yes, probably."

"Will they let you come?"

Mike smiled and said, "Becca, I am still living at home to help save on college expenses, but I'll be twenty years old next month. I think I can decide for myself. I'm not Momma's little boy anymore."

They looked each other straight in the eyes for a moment. Becca realized that she had arrived at a new place in her life.

Mike leaned toward Becca. She smiled and leaned toward him. The kiss was soft and gentle and even though it was only a couple of seconds long, it was perfect. Mike leaned back and smiled, "I'll see you Friday night."

The view out of Becca's window that night was wonderful. The stars gleamed overhead as the falling leaves drifted below. She thought of all her family's concerns: her mom's doubts, her grandma's desire to study, and her dad's rejection of the accusation of heresy ... and Mike's kiss. Trying to put the kiss out of her mind, she prayed, "God, help us as we study. Help us to know the Truth. And God, let us have the courage to stand for the Truth. Thank you for all the wonderful people in my life. In Jesus' Name, Amen."

Chapter 11
Afternoon Tea

Because Thursday was chilly and rainy, Becca and Grandma stayed inside for their afternoon visit. Becca made hot spiced tea and cut pieces of carrot cake for Grandma, Joe and Jim. The boys, who opted to share a soft drink instead of having tea, made quick work of their cake and disappeared to their room, leaving Becca and Grandma at the kitchen table. Becca told Grandma about her date with Mike Friday night, initiating conversation about 'what to wear' and 'how to fix her hair'. As they were talking, they were interrupted by the doorbell. Becca opened the door.

"Hello, Becca!" said Brother Owens enthusiastically.

"Hello, Brother Owens."

She must have had a very puzzled look on her face because Brother Owens continued, "I know this is a surprise, but I was speaking to your dad this morning and he said you would be here with your Grandma this afternoon. I just thought I'd come by and get to know both of you a little better. Is this a convenient time?"

"Yes, of course, come in. Grandma and I are having tea and cake in the kitchen. Please join us," answered Becca.

"That would be wonderful, thank you."

Becca led Brother Owens into the kitchen. "Grandma, we have a visitor. Brother Owens is going to join us for tea and cake." Becca indicated a chair for Brother Owens as she turned to get an extra cup and plate.

Brother Owens stepped around the table to accept the hand which Grandma offered him, "I'm so glad to have this opportunity to get to know you better, Mrs. Elliott," said Brother Owens as he took Grandma's hand in both of his, patting and shaking her hand at the same time. "You and your late husband are a bit of a legend in this part of the state. You are to be admired for all the good work that you have done in the Lord's Kingdom."

Grandma smiled and replied, "Thank you, so much. Of course, George did far more work than I, but I appreciate your thoughtfulness."

"Oh, I never underestimate the influence of a good woman. I truly believe that behind every good man is an even better wife," chuckled Brother Owens.

"Well, I don't know about that 'behind' part," said Grandma with a wry smile and a wink in Becca's direction.

"You are so right! Never underestimate the fairer sex," said Brother Owens, wondering how the conversation had taken this turn. Brother Owens seated himself in the chair that Becca had offered as Becca set tea and cake before him. "Thank you, Becca. This looks great and smells wonderful." Brother Owens sipped his tea and, by a nod and the look on his face, indicated that it was good.

"As I mentioned to Becca at the door, I spoke to Mr. Elliott this morning. Well, actually, he called me. He told me about the study your family is having, and I must tell you that I am very pleased to hear about your interest. Of course, I'm always glad when people study the Bible," he concluded with a bit of a laugh. Grandma and Becca looked at each other and smiled but then focused on Brother Owens.

He continued, "Mr. Elliott said that you were concerned about some of the things I had taught in class and from the pulpit, and well..." Brother Owens paused as a worried look crossed his face as if he didn't know how to continue. He took a deep breath before continuing, "I just want to reassure you. I believe that everything I am teaching is supported by the Bible. I want to preach the truth. I would think that the congregation would want to study the whole Bible to better understand God's plan of salvation, but I have been told that you have some concerns."

A moment of silence fell in the kitchen. Then a glimmer of understanding appeared on Grandma's face. "Brother Owens," said Grandma with concern in her voice, "we are not studying because we are trying to prove that you are wrong, nor are we criticizing your teachings. We are not upset with you. Please put yourself at ease. You have brought some scriptures to our attention that we want to understand better. My son was supposed to ask if you would join our study group and perhaps give us some direction. Did he make you think we were ready to string you up?" Grandma chuckled again and smiled at Brother Owens.

"Oh, no, ma'am. Well, truthfully, I wasn't sure. I understand that there are some folks who are quite upset." Brother Owens smiled regretfully and took another sip of tea.

"Try your cake. It's good," urged Grandma sweetly and Brother Owens obliged.

Grandma continued, "My husband and I often studied together and were sometimes troubled and confused by some passages. To speak frankly, I believe that the Second Coming of Christ happened in the first century, but as time went by, the understanding of that event was lost to most of Christendom. A time came when they misunderstood the nature of the Coming and, therefore, did not recognize that it had already been fulfilled. Taking the New Testament scriptures literally, they concluded, as most people do, that the Second Coming must surely be a future event. Well, as I said, I believe the Coming of our Lord was spiritual and is past; however, I have not found all the pieces to the puzzle, nor can I get the pieces that I have found to fit together properly.

I am interested in hearing your viewpoint. I think you can help me. But, please, don't think that I was the one to start this study. My granddaughter has a keen mind and questions of her own." Grandma's eyes shone with pride as she beamed across at Becca.

Becca asked Brother Owens, "Will you come on Tuesday night? Will you help us with our study?"

"Yes, of course," answered Brother Owens, "Tuesday night? I'll be here." He had a relieved look on his face and a genuine smile of appreciation. As he rose to leave, Grandma said, "Remember, Brother Owens, if you have found the *pearl of truth*, sell all that you have to buy it."

Chapter 12
Football and Stars

Friday night was chilly and clear – excellent football weather. With Mom's help and Grandma's approval, Becca was finally ready. Mike had only a short wait with Becca's dad in the living room. When Becca entered the room, they were discussing the evening news.

"Hi," said Mike, standing when Becca joined them.

As she handed Mike her jacket, Becca turned to Dad and said, "I'll be in by eleven o'clock, Dad."

"OK, Sis," responded Dad.

As they pulled away in the car, Mike smiled at Becca and asked, "Hungry?"

"Yes, I am," admitted Becca, "I don't eat much lunch at school."

"Do you want burgers or pizza?" asked Mike.

"Either is fine with me," said Becca.

"No, you must choose: burgers or pizza?" insisted Mike.

"OK, then, pizza." said Becca.

Mike said, "Great, then, I choose Joe's Pizza at the mall."

"Great," agreed Becca. "How is school going?"

They talked for a while about both of their school experiences and a little about Becca's college plans. "I really haven't made up my mind," said Becca. "I've thought about teaching, nursing, or psychology. I really don't know."

"You don't have to decide on a major in your first year. Just take the required general courses," suggested Mike.

"Good idea," agreed Becca.

As they were being seated in a booth at Joe's Pizza, Mike gave their order to the waitress.

While they waited for the pizza, Becca told Mike about Brother Owens' visit. "I think he was really worried that we were questioning his teaching – criticizing it or calling it heresy."

"Well, I know some people, my folks included, are upset," said Mike. "I don't really think they know whether it is right or wrong; they just know it's different from what they have always been taught. The main ring leader stirring the others up is Mr. Collin. He previously attended a congregation which split over this issue. He is the one calling it *heresy*."

"So," said Becca, "if that congregation split over this issue, then some people must have believed it's the truth and others disagreed."

"Or, at least," added Mike, "some thought it should be studied and others thought it should be shut down."

"Where was this congregation?" asked Becca.

"Cedarvale."

"Really!" exclaimed Becca, "I didn't know that. Well, no wonder that group of people went to meet with the Cedarvale leaders. I'll bet they were the ones who wanted to shut it down."

"Exactly," confirmed Mike.

"So," asked Becca with concern, "what do you think is going to happen?"

"I think," said Mike, "that if Brother Owens continues to teach this viewpoint in class or from the pulpit, this group of people will apply pressure for him to be fired. Our congregation has five leaders and three of them visited with Cedarvale."

Was Brother Owens at Cedarvale when that congregation split?" asked Becca.

"No," said Mike, "I don't know that preacher's name, but it wasn't Brother Owens.

"Well," continued Becca, "I don't know the truth on this issue. But it's wrong to deny people the opportunity to study it if they wish to. Grandma really wants to hear what Brother Owens has to say. She wants to study with him and so do I."

"Yeah, me too," said Mike with a expression on his face that said 'I hope we get to'.

When their pizza arrived, the subject changed to more casual topics such as the chances of winning tonight's game.

* * *

When Mike and Becca entered the stadium, the band had just finished playing *The Star Spangled Banner* and had begun the school's fight song. They hurried to the student section. Becca started down a row which had seats available, only to discover that she was headed straight for Jenny. She hadn't seen Jenny or talked to her on the phone over the past couple of weeks. They had a class together before lunch, but Jenny hadn't waited for Becca, and Becca had not been able to locate Jenny once she got to the cafeteria.

As Becca took the seat beside Jenny, she noticed that Jenny looked apprehensive, but Becca greeted her with enthusiasm. "Hi, Jenny! It's so good to see you."

"Hi," answered Jenny but she kept her attention carefully focused on the ballgame.

After the next football play, Becca tried again, "I've really been missing you. Are you doing OK?"

"Yes, thanks," answered Jenny still keeping her eyes trained forward on the field.

Becca decided to take this opportunity to ask what was wrong between them. "Jenny,"

Becca insisted, "We have been such good friends for so long. Can't we be friends anymore?" The concern and hurt was evident in Becca's voice.

Jenny was also showing signs of being upset, but she kept her eyes straight ahead, and blurted out, "No, I don't think we can."

"Have I hurt your feeling in some way?"

"No."

"What is wrong then?" asked Becca

"My dad says I can't have anything to do with people who believe in that heresy," answered Jenny.

"Jenny, I don't know if I believe in the teaching or not. I just want to study it. I want to be able to make up my own mind." Becca paused and waited for Jenny to answer. Jenny did not reply.

Becca turned back to Mike. He had been listening to the girls and he empathized with both of them. They were each losing a friend for no good reason. When Mike saw a tear slide down Becca's cheek, he took her hand in his to let her know he was there for her. In a couple of minutes, when Becca had recovered her composure, she directed her attention to the game and to Mike. They made the most of the game – cheering and chanting with the crowd. As Mike had predicted, the home team won.

While they were making their way out of the crowded stadium, Becca glanced at her watch, noting that the time was only 9:45. She wondered, 'Would Mike take her straight home?'

After they were both in the car, Mike turned to Becca and asked, "How do you like star gazing?"

"Oh, I like it a lot! I star gaze from my bedroom window," answered Becca with enthusiasm.

"OK, then," said Mike. "Here we go."

Mike drove through the college campus to the park on the far side. He explained, "There's an old outdoor amphitheater in this park and, because there isn't much lighting out there, it is an excellent place for star gazing."

Looking out into the dark park, Becca became concerned. Seeing the worried expression flit across her face, Mike added, "Don't worry. I expect that several people will be out here on a clear night like this. David will probably have his telescope set up." Mike got a blanket from the trunk of the car, saying, "This will cushion the cold stone seats of the amphitheater."

Mike's prediction was right. Several people were inside the amphitheater. Two guys were working with a telescope on the old stage area and several couples were seated throughout the semicircle of stone seats .

Looking up into the night sky, Becca immediately saw a shooting star. She closed her eyes to wish but could not decide what to wish for. Should she wish for her friendship with Jenny to be restored? Should she wish for her relationship with Mike to go well? Before she could complete a wish, Mike was directing her to a place to sit. Becca helped Mike fold the blanket so that they could sit on part of it and lean their backs against part of it resting on the stone row behind.

The night sky stretched out above them. After a couple of comments about the beauty and majesty of the skies, they sat silently staring into space. Again, a shooting star shot across the sky. Mike reached and found Becca's hand. Because Becca had not needed her jacket at the ballgame, she had left it in the car; but the night was getting colder and she shivered. Mike encouraged, "Here, scoot over closer."

As Becca moved closer to Mike, he raised his arm so that she was cradled by his arm at the shoulder. Mike wrapped his arms around Becca, gently pulling her closer.

"Better?" asked Mike.

"Better," agreed Becca.

Mike and Becca began to point out the constellations that each knew. They also talked about the legends behind the constellations. Together, they knew quite a lot.

Finally, Becca had to confess that she was cold. "Mike, I'm sorry, but I'm getting really cold."

"Yeah, me, too," admitted Mike.

Mike stood up first; then helped Becca up. Pulling her directly into him, he enclosed her in both arms. At first, she felt self-conscious being held by Mike in front of other people; however, no one seemed to be noticing them. She felt him kiss her hair. She turned her face up to him and they kissed, first, a soft short kiss, then a longer kiss. Mike released his hold on Becca and bent to pick up the blanket. "We'd better go," Mike said. "It's really getting cold."

As they drove back through the campus, the car heater warmed them. Mike pulled up at Becca's house. Becca waited, expecting Mike would get her door. However, leaning on the console between their seats, Mike said, "I had a good time tonight."

"Me, too," said Becca.

"Can I have another kiss?" asked Mike.

Becca leaned to Mike. The kiss was soft and short. Mike smiled as he turned to get out. Mike opened Becca's door. As they walked up to the porch, Mike jammed his hands in his jean pockets trying to warm them. Before opening the door, Becca turned to Mike and whispered "Goodnight."

"Goodnight," answered Mike. "I'll call you."

"OK," said Becca. As Becca opened the door and disappeared inside, Mike ran back to his car.

* * *

From the window in Becca's room, Becca prayed, "Dear Father, help me find a way to keep Jenny as a friend. Thank you for bringing Mike into my life. And Father, thank you for bringing Brother Owens to us. Help us to understand your truth. In Jesus' Name, Amen."

Chapter 13
Brother Owens' First Assignment

Sunday morning was overcast and cold. The family arrived at church and dispersed to their various classes; but Becca lingered in the foyer for Mike. He had telephoned on Saturday afternoon. They discussed the previous night, agreeing that they had each had a great time. Then Mike had turned the conservation to Jenny. "Becca, I know you are upset about Jenny, but I understand the situation that Jenny is in. It is difficult for her to go against her parents' wishes. They have a close family just as you do. If your dad told you not to do something or not to associate with someone, I know it would be very difficult for you to disobey him. Jenny is in the same situation. Her dad thinks he is doing the right thing by protecting Jenny from learning about a doctrine which he believes is heresy. Jenny's heart is probably breaking because she can't have you for a friend just now. Don't be too hard on her; maybe she will come around in time."

"I hadn't looked at it like that," said Becca. "Thanks, Mike. With your parents' opposition, I suppose it is difficult for you, too?"

"Yes," continued Mike, "it is. But, remember, I understand that I am old enough to make up my own mind. Not that I like disagreeing with my parents, but I need to decide for myself. It is just like becoming a Christian. You shouldn't become a Christian just because your parents want you to. You have to want it for yourself. Jenny is just having trouble thinking independently from her parents."

"Yeah," replied Becca.

"Becca," Mike started, then paused.

"What, Mike?" asked Becca.

"Would it be all right with you if I visited with Jenny to help her understand what is going on? I understand what she is feeling, and, well, maybe I can help. Perhaps I can work out a compromise to help you two be friends, without Jenny's feeling as if she is disobeying her dad."

"Oh, Mike, would you do that?" asked Becca. "That might help a lot. It is so nice of you to help," Becca paused and then added, "and to care."

"Of course I care," answered Mike. "I would do anything I possibly could to help you."

"Thanks," replied Becca, smiling on her end of the phone.

Mike continued, "Let's meet in the foyer in the morning before going to class. OK?"

"OK."

* * *

Becca had waited in the foyer only a couple of minutes when Mike arrived with his parents. He promptly brought them toward Becca.

Mike began, "Mom and Dad, this is Becca Elliott, Frank and Elizabeth Elliott's daughter."

Mike's mom replied, "Oh, yes, we've watched Becca grow up.

Mike continued, "Becca, these are my parents."

"How do you do, Mr. and Mrs. Gibbons," Becca said, extending her hand to Mrs. Gibbons.

Mrs. Gibbons took Becca's hand and said, "In fact, I had Becca in Bible class when she was in the third grade."

"Yes, that's right," replied Becca. "I had forgotten."

Becca extended her hand to Mr. Gibbons as he said, "Nice to meet you, Becca."

"Well, we'd better get to class," said Mike.

"It was nice to meet you," said Becca as she and Mike turned to go to class.

As they made their way across the foyer, they were greeted by Brother Owens. "Good morning, Becca and Mike! I am looking forward to our study Tuesday night. In fact, I've made a list of scriptures which I would like everyone to read before we meet. If you will stop by my office after services, I will give it to you."

"Certainly," replied Mike.

"Thank you," said Becca as she and Mike moved on.

Class had already started by the time Becca got to her room. She quietly took a seat, one chair away from Jenny.

Mr. Simms announced, "We are in Matthew 25, Becca."

Becca found Matthew 25 and directed her attention to Mr. Simms. He did not refer to the questions she had asked last week but started on the parable of the ten virgins – five of whom were not ready when the bridegroom came. Verse 13 concluded the parable with the warning to *'Watch therefore, for you know neither the day nor the hour in which the Son of Man is coming'*. Becca wanted to bring up her question about *that generation* again, but she didn't. She would save her questions for Brother Owens.

Becca and Mike sat together during worship service. The lesson was from Isaiah 53 in which Christ as the lamb was led to the slaughter. He opened not His mouth, but bore the sins of the world on the cross. Brother Owens' appeal at the end of the sermon was for sinners to accept the sacrifice of Christ and the grace and love He offers them.

Becca located her mother after they were dismissed to tell her that she would come to the car as soon as she could. First, she had to wait for Brother Owens to get a list of scriptures for them to study. It took several minutes for Brother Owens to shake hands with everyone who was leaving. Mike and Becca waited quietly nearby. Becca heard Mr. Collin say to Brother Owens, "Good lesson this morning, Brother Owens." Becca and Mike looked at each other and smiled. Becca was glad Mr. Collin was happy.

Finally, when the last family had gone, Brother Owens saw Becca and Mike waiting for him. "Oh, yes," he said, "I'm sorry you had to wait. Let's get that list right now."

With the list in hand, Becca and Mike went down the front steps. There at the bottom of the steps were both sets of their parents. They seemed to be having a friendly visit and, when they saw Becca and Mike, everyone smiled up at them. Becca's dad said, "Here they are now."

Becca apologized, "I'm sorry it took so long. Thanks for waiting."

After goodbyes were said, Mike and his parents went toward the parking lot. Mike turned and made a gesture with his hand to his ear that signaled 'I'll call you'.

Dad had driven the car around to the front of the building. Grandma and the boys were waiting patiently, or at least Grandma was waiting patiently. The boys made an ugly face at Becca and were secretly pleased when she playfully returned it.

When Mike called that afternoon, Becca had the list of scriptures to read to him. "Are you ready?" asked Becca. "It's a pretty long list."

"I'm ready," replied Mike.

Becca read slowly, "Genesis 3, Genesis 12:1-4, Genesis 17:1-8, Genesis 22:15-19, Genesis 28:10-15, Genesis 49:1-2 & 8-12, Deuteronomy 32 and Judges 2:10-12." Becca paused, "Did you get all of that?"

"Wow, yes, I think I did," answered Mike.

"Would you like to come over tonight so we could do this reading together?" suggested Becca.

"I would really like to, but I have some assignments for school that are due tomorrow," answered Mike. "I think I will be working from now until late." Then he added, "Now you know the truth – I'm a procrastinator."

"I'll see you Tuesday, then," said Becca.

"Tuesday, it is," said Mike.

"Goodbye," said Becca, waiting for Mike to say goodbye.

"Becca?" started Mike.

"Yes," answered Becca.

"Never mind," said Mike. "Good-bye."

Wondering what Mike had decided not to say, Becca copied the list for Dad, Mom and Grandma. As she handed the list to Dad, he suggested that she might help Grandma with the reading because of her recent episodes of dizziness. Becca asked Grandma if she would like her to read the passages to her.

"Oh, yes," said Grandma. "That would be a great help. Thank you, Dear."

"How are you feeling, Grandma?" Becca asked.

Grandma replied, "I feel better in the mornings. By the afternoon, sometimes my eyes start to blur and, when my eyes are open, the room spins around, making me sick at my stomach. I'll just lie here with my eyes closed while you read."

Becca spent an hour with Grandma, reading and talking about the passages.

They agreed that Tuesday night's lesson should be an interesting study.

That night at her window, Becca prayed, "Heavenly Father, help us as we study to understand your Word. Thank you for bringing Brother Owens to us. And, Father, be with Grandma and help her to feel better. In Jesus' Name, Amen."

Chapter 14
Tuesday Night Number Three

For the Tuesday night study, Becca moved to sit next to Mike. Mom was sharing the opposite side with Grandma, so Frank and Brother Owens seated themselves at each end of the table.

"Please, Brother Owens, take the lead," suggested Frank.

Brother Owens nodded in acceptance and said, "Thank you. First, I would like to know what your questions are."

Frank volunteered Becca, "Becca, why don't you tell him your original question?"

"OK," said Becca as she tried to decide how to phrase her thoughts "My Grandpa Elliott – I guess all the other preachers I had ever heard – preached that some day there will be a Resurrection and Judgment. If you are found faithful or worthy, I guess, then you go to Heaven with all the saved. But, when I listen to you preach, you seem to be saying that Christians should not fear death because when they die, they go immediately to Heaven. That would mean that they are not waiting for a Resurrection or a Judgment. When I asked Dad about it, he said that you had been teaching that concept in the adult class, too, so we decided we wanted to study the subject at home. When Grandma heard what we were studying, she wanted to join in on it, too. We aren't sure how to interpret some scriptures that seem to say 'Christ came in that generation', like Matthew 24. I guess Grandma has more of an opinion than any of us. She told you that the other day."

"Yes, she did," chuckled Brother Owens. "OK, I would like to start with the passages I listed for Becca and Mike on Sunday. I hope everyone had time to read them. If you have a question or something you want to add during our study, just speak up."

Everyone nodded in agreement. Mike asked, "Brother Owens if it is all right with you, I would like to record tonight's session. I have been talking to my parents about studying with us, but they wouldn't come with me tonight. Maybe I can get them to listen to the lesson on tape."

Brother Owens indicated that making a recording of the lesson would be all right and he began, "I believe our study starts in the Garden of Eden; that is why I assigned Genesis 3."

> *Gen 3:1 Now the serpent was more cunning than any beast of the field which the LORD God had made. And he said to the woman, "Has God indeed said, 'You shall not eat of every tree of the garden'?"*
>
> *2 And the woman said to the serpent, "We may eat the fruit of the trees of the garden; 3 but of the fruit of the tree which is in the midst of the garden, God has said, 'You shall not eat it, nor shall you touch it, lest you die.'"*
>
> *4 Then the serpent said to the woman, "You will not surely die. 5 For God knows that in the day you eat of it your eyes will be opened, and you will be like God, knowing good and evil."*
>
> *6 So when the woman saw that the tree was good for food, that it was pleasant to the eyes, and a tree desirable to make one wise, she took of its fruit and ate. She also gave to her husband with her, and he ate. 7 Then the eyes of both of them were opened, and they knew that they were naked; and they sewed fig leaves together and*

made themselves coverings.

8 And they heard the sound of the LORD God walking in the garden in the cool of the day, and Adam and his wife hid themselves from the presence of the LORD God among the trees of the garden.

9 Then the LORD God called to Adam and said to him, "Where are you?"

10 So he said, "I heard Your voice in the garden, and I was afraid because I was naked; and I hid myself."

11 And He said, "Who told you that you were naked? Have you eaten from the tree of which I commanded you that you should not eat?"

12 Then the man said, "The woman whom You gave to be with me, she gave me of the tree, and I ate."

13 And the LORD God said to the woman, "What is this you have done?"

The woman said, "The serpent deceived me, and I ate."

14 So the LORD God said to the serpent:

> *"Because you have done this, You are cursed more than all cattle, And more than every beast of the field; On your belly you shall go, And you shall eat dust All the days of your life. 15 And I will put enmity between you and the woman, And between your seed and her Seed; He shall bruise your head, And you shall bruise His heel."*

16 To the woman He said:

"I will greatly multiply your sorrow and your conception; In pain you shall bring forth children; Your desire shall be for your husband, And he shall rule over you."

17 Then to Adam He said, "Because you have heeded the voice of your wife, and have eaten from the tree of which I commanded you, saying, 'You shall not eat of it':

"Cursed is the ground for your sake; In toil you shall eat of it All the days of your life. 18 Both thorns and thistles it shall bring forth for you, And you shall eat the herb of the field. 19 In the sweat of your face you shall eat bread Till you return to the ground, For out of it you were taken; For dust you are, And to dust you shall return."

20 And Adam called his wife's name Eve, because she was the mother of all living.

21 Also for Adam and his wife the LORD God made tunics of skin, and clothed them.

22 Then the LORD God said, "Behold, the man has become like one of Us, to know good and evil. And now, lest he put out his hand and take also of the tree of life, and eat, and live forever" — 23 therefore the LORD God sent him out of the garden of Eden to till the ground from which he was taken. 24 So He drove out the man; and He placed cherubim at the east of the garden of Eden, and a flaming sword which turned every way, to guard the way to the tree of life.

"I wanted you to read this passage in Genesis," Brother Owens began, "because one of the key ideas that will allow everything else to make more sense is the definition of *death*. Adam and Eve both sinned when they ate of the forbidden fruit. The devil tempted them with the idea that they could be like God, knowing good from evil, and so they bit. God had said that if they ate they would die: '*in the day you eat you will surely die*'. So here is the first big question. Did they die that day? Or did God lie?"

There was silence for a moment before Frank spoke up, "I don't think I would ever be comfortable saying God lied; but they didn't die that day. I've heard some preachers say *they began to die that day,* because if they had not sinned and had stayed in the garden they would have never died."

"Well, let's ask this question," suggested Brother Owens. "Is there more than one kind of death? Does the Bible mention a death other than physical death?"

Mike volunteered, "I've heard about spiritual death."

"Can you be spiritually dead and physically alive?" asked Brother Owens.

Mike answered again, "Yes, I think so. You can be physically alive; but if you are not a Christian - if you are not *in Christ* - then you are spiritually dead."

"Can everyone agree with that?" asked Brother Owens as he looked around the group. "I think Mike is exactly right. There is physical death and there is spiritual death. We know Adam and Eve did not die physically that day. Is there any evidence or suggestion in the text that they died spiritually?"

Becca answered, "God put them out of the garden."

Grandma added, "The importance of that is that they were no longer in the presence of God."

"Is God more concerned about our souls or our physical bodies?" asked Brother Owens. "Did Christ die to give us spiritual life or physical life?"

Everyone agreed that both God and Christ were more concerned with spiritual life than with physical life.

"OK, then," said Brother Owens. "Man has a problem. When man sins, man becomes spiritually dead. Does this passage in Genesis 3 suggest that there will be an answer – a solution – to this problem?"

Frank answered, "Well, in verse 15, God says that the Seed of woman will crush Satan's head. If this Seed of woman can make people spiritually alive, Satan will be crushed."

Everyone smiled and nodded their heads in agreement.

"Now, as I'm sure all of you know," said Brother Owens, "God set in motion His plan to save man. Let's turn to the next passage, Genesis 12:1-4."

> *Gen 12:1-3 Now the LORD had said to Abram:*
>> *"Get out of your country,*
>> *From your family*
>> *And from your father's house,*
>> *To a land that I will show you.*
>> *2 I will make you a great nation;*
>> *I will bless you*
>> *And make your name great;*
>> *And you shall be a blessing.*
>> *3 I will bless those who bless you,*
>> *And I will curse him who curses you;*
>> *And in you all the families of the earth shall be blessed."*

When everyone had located the passage, Brother Owens asked, "Why do you think I chose this scripture?"

Everyone was a bit surprised when Beth spoke, "Because it was through the descendants of Abraham that the Christ would come."

"Exactly," said Brother Owens with a smile in Beth's direction. "What are the promises that God made to Abraham?"

Mike paraphrased, "*I will make you a great nation; I will bless you and make your name great; and you shall be a blessing. I will bless those who bless you. And I will curse him who curses you; and in you all the families of the earth shall be blessed.*"

"Thank you, Mike," said Brother Owens. "Becca, will you look at Genesis 17:1-8 and pick out the promises listed there?"

> *Gen 17:1 When Abram was ninety-nine years old, the LORD appeared to Abram and said to him, "I am Almighty God; walk before Me and be blameless. 2 And I will make My covenant*

between Me and you, and will multiply you exceedingly." 3 Then Abram fell on his face, and God talked with him, saying: 4 "As for Me, behold, My covenant is with you, and you shall be a father of many nations. 5 No longer shall your name be called Abram, but your name shall be Abraham; for I have made you a father of many nations. 6 I will make you exceedingly fruitful; and I will make nations of you, and kings shall come from you. 7 And I will establish My covenant between Me and you and your descendants after you in their generations, for an everlasting covenant, to be God to you and your descendants after you. 8 Also I give to you and your descendants after you the land in which you are a stranger, all the land of Canaan, as an everlasting possession; and I will be their God."

Becca responded, *"I will make My Covenant between you and me, and will multiply you exceedingly. You shall be the father of many nations. I will make you exceeding fruitful; I will make nations of you, and kings shall come from you. I will give to you and your descendants after you the land in which you are a stranger, all the land of Canaan, as an everlasting possession."*

"Frank, would you turn to Genesis 22:15-19 and pick out the promises there?"

Gen 22:15 Then the Angel of the LORD called to Abraham a second time out of heaven, 16 and said: "By Myself I have sworn, says the LORD, because you have done this thing, and have not withheld your son, your only son — 17 blessing I will bless you, and multiplying I will multiply your descendants as the stars of the heaven and as the sand which is on the seashore; and your descendants shall possess the gate of their enemies. 18 In your seed all the nations of the earth shall be blessed, because you have obeyed My voice." 19 So Abraham returned to his young men, and they rose and went together to Beersheba; and Abraham dwelt at Beersheba.

Frank answered, "*I will bless you; I will multiply your descendants;, your descendants shall possess the gate of their enemies*; and in verse eighteen, '*In your seed all the nations of the earth shall be blessed…*'."

"These are the promises made to Abraham on three different occasions. There are several parts to these promises and they are not all fulfilled at the same time. Ishmael was a son of Abraham who became a great nation. Esau was the grandson of Abraham, and his people became a great nation. Four hundred years after this promise, Moses led tens-of-thousands of Israelites, the descendants of Abraham, out of Egypt. Under the direction of Joshua and with the help of God, they drove out their enemies. The scriptures state that they possessed The Promised Land. Therefore, the promise of *great nations* has been fulfilled and the promise of *possessing the land* has also been fulfilled. But when were *all* the families of the earth blessed? Has this prophecy been fulfilled yet?"

Beth answered again, "I think it was fulfilled when Christ died on the cross."

Brother Owens asked, "Yes, the crucifixion is a very important event, but the Day of Pentecost was important too, wasn't it? Yet even on the Day of Pentecost, the invitation was extended to Jews only. The gospel invitation did not include the Gentiles until the pouring out of the Holy Spirit on the household of Cornelius. Some Bible scholars place that event some years after Pentecost.

Beth thought a moment and replied, "I was always taught that the Old Covenant was fulfilled at the cross."

"One of the main purposes of our study," said Brother Owens, "is going to be to determine what prophecies to Israel had to be fulfilled and when these prophecies were fulfilled. Or are there prophecies which have not yet been fulfilled?" Brother Owens paused for a moment before continuing, "Let's look at the next passage. Remember, we are trying to trace the path of God's plan for solving man's problem of spiritual death."

Brother Owens directed their attention to Genesis 28:14-15.

Gen 28:14 Also your descendants shall be as the dust of the earth; you shall spread abroad to the west and the east, to the north and the south; and in you and in your seed all the families of the earth shall be blessed. 15 Behold, I am with you and will keep you wherever you go, and will bring you back to this land; for I will not leave you until I have done what I have spoken to you."

"In this passage, the promises made to Abraham are being repeated to Jacob. In verse 14, we see God's promise to bless all nations. Then, verse 15 says, *'I will not leave you until I have done what I have spoken to you'*. God was not speaking about Jacob exclusively but was referring to the descendants of Jacob, the Israelites. God said that He would not leave Israel, His chosen people, until He had done all that He promised. God would not leave Israel until all the nations of the earth received the promised blessing." Brother Owens paused momentarily, "So, consider this question. Will God then leave His chosen people, the Israelites, when all the promises are fulfilled?"

There was silence for several moments before Grandma answered, "When all of Israel's promises are fulfilled, the New Covenant will fully come into effect. The people of God will be the ones who answer the gospel call – those who believe and obey Jesus. If Israel does not answer the gospel call, God will bring judgment and destruction on them. They will no longer be His people."

Brother Owens moved on to the next verse because it blended so well with what Grandma had said. "Genesis 49 is a prophecy that reveals when that will happen. Look at verses 1 and 2. Beth," said Brother Owens, "would you read those verses for us?"

She read, *"And Jacob called his sons and said, "Gather together, that I may tell you what shall befall you in the last days: Gather together and hear, you sons of Jacob, and listen to Israel your father.""*

Brother Owens spoke a little more enthusiastically, "Did you hear that? *'What shall befall you'* when?"

Becca answered, *"In the last days."*

"Exactly," said Brother Owens. *"In the last days.* It is going to be very important to our study to understand when these last days are. The last days of what?"

Brother Owens had not intended that question to be answered just yet. He thought it would take more study before they discovered the answer, but Becca spoke up to suggest, "I think it is talking about the last days of the Israelites, the last days of the Old Covenant."

"That may be the correct answer, Becca," began Brother Owens, "but some scholars suggest that it means the last days of the Christian age or even the last days of the physical world. As we continue our study over the next few weeks, perhaps we will find the Biblical answer. Now, let's look at the rest of this passage. Brother Owens resumed, "Frank, would you read verse 10?"

Frank read, *"The scepter shall not depart from Judah, nor a lawgiver from between his feet, until Shiloh comes; and to Him shall be the obedience of the people."*

Brother Owens continued, "Who is this Shiloh?"

Grandma answered, "That was one of the names that Israel used to refer to the Messiah."

Brother Owens continued, "In scripture, God promised that authority would stay with Judah until the Messiah came. Does everyone know that Judah is one of the tribes of Israel?"

Everyone nodded in agreement.

"One of the questions that will come up is this: which Coming of Christ are we talking about? Are we referring to His coming in the flesh and being crucified, or are we talking about the Second Coming?

Let's not answer that yet. Let me point out that all the passages that we have studied thus far were all prophesied before the nation of Israel was led to Mt. Sinai to receive the Law of Moses. Even before the Old Covenant was established, God was talking about the Messiah and the New Covenant to come."

Brother Owens glanced at his notes and said, "Let's review the history of Israel. Because of a famine, Jacob's family moved to Egypt, where his son, Joseph, was second only to the Pharaoh. However, many years after Joseph's death, a Pharaoh came into power and enslaved the Israelites, forcing them to make bricks for his building projects. God sent Moses to deliver the people. Even after many plagues, Pharaoh still would not let the Israelites go; therefore, God sent the worst plague of all. Let's call it the *death of the firstborn*. During all the other plagues, the Israelites had not been plagued." Everyone laughed at the humorous use of words. "I mean the Israelites had not been affected. But the *death of the first born* was a plague that would affect even them if they did not follow God's specific instructions. The Passover was instituted for the first time. Briefly, each family had to kill a lamb without blemish and put its blood on the doorpost. All households with blood on the doorposts would then be safe from the plague of *the death of the first born*.

After losing his own son, Pharaoh finally let the people go. Moses led the Israelites out of Egypt and to Mt. Sinai on their way to the Promised Land. On the journey, the Israelites murmured and rebelled in spite of the miracles Moses preformed to satisfy their complaints. I mention the complaining and miracles because, even though Abraham, Isaac, and Jacob had been faithful to God, their descendants were not always faithful. On the road to Sinai, they frequently complained about their conditions. God often answered their complaints with miracles; but they just didn't seem to appreciate that their God was the only true God. They sometimes said that they wished they were back as slaves in Egypt. God called them a *stiffed necked people*. Even while Moses was on the mountain receiving the Law from God, the people sinned by casting a golden calf and calling it their 'god'. One of the readings that I included is the 'Song of Moses', Deuteronomy 32.

Before Moses died, through the inspiration of God, he prophesied the future and the end of Israel. In brief, the scripture promises to the Israelites, '*if you keep My law, I will cause you to prosper,* but *if you fail to keep My law, I will destroy you.*' The end of the song revealed that there will ultimately be rejoicing for the Gentiles."

"Is that the blessing of all the nations?" asked Grandma.

"That's right," continued Brother Owens, "and it was to come *in the last days* that Jacob foretold. Under the leadership of Joshua, the people conquered and possessed all the land they had been promised. However, after Joshua died, the people again became unfaithful to God. Mike, would you read Judges 2 verse 10?"

"Yes, sir," answered Mike.

"*When all that generation had been gathered to their fathers, another generation arose after them who did not know the Lord nor the work which He had done for Israel.*"

"Read through to verse 12, please," added Brother Owens.

Mike continued,

"*Then the children of Israel did evil in the sight of the Lord, and served the Baals; and they forsook the Lord God of their fathers, who had brought them out of the land of Egypt; and they followed other gods from among the gods of the people who were all around them, and they provoked the Lord to anger.*"

Brother Owens continued, "This was typical of Israel. Under the leadership of faithful leaders like King David, the people repented and served God. In such times, God blessed them and made them prosper. Whenever they fell away again, God cursed them and let their enemies conquer them and use them as slaves. Finally, there came a time when the ten northern tribes, all the tribes except Judah and Benjamin, declared that they wanted to have nothing to do with Jerusalem. The nation of Israel split into two nations, each with its own king. Eventually, the northern kingdom became so sinful by serving other gods that God stated that He divorced or disowned them. He declared that they were no longer His people. They were carried off into captivity in foreign lands and there intermarried with other nations, thus losing their special identity. They then became known as the 'ten lost tribes'. God continued with the Kingdom of Judah and preserved her, even though Judah was, at times, just as sinful as the lost tribes. Why was God so longsuffering toward Judah?"

Even after several moments, no one had answered so Brother Owens continued, "Because God had a plan and He would allow nothing to prevent the completion of His plan. Through the tribe of Judah, He had promised to bring the Messiah. Remember, *'the scepter will not depart from Judah, before Shiloh comes'*."

"Let's return to our first idea, the problem of spiritual death. What were the Israelites supposed to do when they sinned?"

Beth answered, "They had to bring animal sacrifices and, once every year on the Day of Atonement, the high priest had to carry the blood into the Most Holy Place."

"What does the New Testament tell us about the blood of bulls and goats?" asked Brother Owens.

"It is not possible that the blood of bulls and goats could take away sins," quoted Frank.

"Exactly," said Brother Owens. "Hebrews 10:4: *'For it is not possible that the blood of bulls and goats could take away sins.'* But that is what they were to do. You see, God was impressing on them the fact that sin results in spiritual death, just as it had for Adam and Eve. Because sin results in spiritual death, death is required to atone for sin."

"Well, this has been enough for one night. Thank you so much for asking me to come. It is a pleasure studying with such good Bible students."

Beth jumped up, exclaiming, "Oh! I almost forgot. I baked a coffee cake for tonight."

Frank said, "Hey, that sounds good. Bring it out. Becca, invite your brothers down for cake."

Brother Owens, who had started to rise, sat down immediately, saying, "Cake would be great."

The boys, excited about cake and milk, pulled up extra chairs to the table. Beth sliced cake while Becca delivered it around the table.

"What topic are we going to cover next week, Brother Owens?" asked Grandma.

"Next week," began Brother Owens, "I thought we should study some of the major prophecies made to Israel about the New Covenant."

"Good, good," said Grandma. "That's the part I want to study, the prophecies. Were the prophecies for Israel's future or the church's future?"

"Mrs. Elliott," said Brother Owens to Grandma, "that is an important question. I have a list of scriptures here for everyone to read. There are quite a few here but I think it is important that we get a comprehensive look at several prophecies so that we can see their harmony and consistent message." The list included: Isaiah 25:6-9, Isaiah 26:19-21, Isaiah 62:10-11, Isaiah 66:5-17, Ezekiel 37 Hosea 13, Daniel 12, and the book of Joel. Brother Owens had made a note on the bottom of the paper, "While you read, watch for references to the *Coming of the Lord*, the *Resurrection of Israel*, and the *Judgment of the world*."

Everyone let out a fake moan at the homework assignment, but they were actually enjoying the study because Brother Owens was a good teacher, easy to follow. He taught in plain language that they could understand.

After a few moments of visiting, Mike remembered that he had a school assignment that still had to be finished tonight.

As he began to explain that he needed to go, Frank apologized, "I'm sorry, I hope we didn't keep you too late."

"No, sir," said Mike, "I still have time to get the assignment. It's only nine o'clock. There are still three hours before midnight and midnight is early for most college students. Thank you for the delicious cake, Mrs. Elliott. Thank you for studying with us, Brother Owens. Goodnight everyone."

Becca walked to the front porch with Mike. After one quick kiss, he was gone. Brother Owens finished saying his farewells in the kitchen and was soon on his way, also.

Grandma remarked, "Well, that young man's bedtime might not be till midnight, but mine was thirty minutes ago."

"You seem to be feeling better this evening, Grandma," commented Becca as she accompanied her to her room.

"Yes, I think that the opportunity to study with Brother Owens must have perked me up a bit."

"Do you need my help, Grandma?" asked Becca.

"No, I'll be fine, dear. Thank you," answered Grandma.

Becca returned to the kitchen to help her mom, but saw that she had already cleared everything away. Mom smiled at her, "Thanks, but no help needed here. Goodnight, Sweetie."

Reflecting on the evening, Becca stood at her window for a long time that night. She had enjoyed the challenge of their Bible study. She liked Brother Owens. She was proud of her family. Brother Owens had praised them as good Bible students. She thought about Mike, happy that she felt so comfortable with him. She thought about his parents; they were really nice people. She hoped they would listen to the tape of tonight's lesson and possibly join the group next week. She turned her thoughts wistfully to Jenny. She wished Jenny and Jenny's folks would study with them, too. Becca didn't know how the study was going to end. She wondered what she would conclude. Has Christ already come and, if so, what does that mean? She didn't know yet. But one thing she did know: it was right to study. She remembered the verse about the Bereans: *'...they searched the scriptures daily, whether those things were so.'* (Acts 17:11)

"Thank you, God, for the people in my life who are willing to search the scriptures. In Jesus' Name, Amen."

Becca crawled into bed with her Bible to reread the Song of Moses as found in Deuteronomy 32.

> *"Give ear, O heavens, and I will speak;*
> *And hear, O earth, the words of my mouth.*
> *2 Let my teaching drop as the rain,*
> *My speech distill as the dew,*
> *As raindrops on the tender herb,*
> *And as showers on the grass.*
> *3 For I proclaim the name of the LORD:*
> *Ascribe greatness to our God.*
> *4 He is the Rock, His work is perfect;*
> *For all His ways are justice,*
> *A God of truth and without injustice;*
> *Righteous and upright is He.*
> *5 "They have corrupted themselves;*
> *They are not His children,*
> *Because of their blemish:*
> *A perverse and crooked generation.*
> *6 Do you thus deal with the LORD,*
> *O foolish and unwise people?*
> *Is He not your Father, who bought you?*
> *Has He not made you and established you?*
> *7 "Remember the days of old,*
> *Consider the years of many generations.*

Ask your father, and he will show you;
Your elders, and they will tell you:
8 When the Most High divided their inheritance to the nations,
When He separated the sons of Adam,
He set the boundaries of the peoples
According to the number of the children of Israel.
9 For the LORD's portion is His people;
Jacob is the place of His inheritance.
10 "He found him in a desert land
And in the wasteland, a howling wilderness;
He encircled him, He instructed him,
He kept him as the apple of His eye.
11 As an eagle stirs up its nest, Hovers over its young,
Spreading out its wings, taking them up,
Carrying them on its wings,
12 So the LORD alone led him,
And there was no foreign god with him.
13 "He made him ride in the heights of the earth,
That he might eat the produce of the fields;
He made him draw honey from the rock,
And oil from the flinty rock;
14 Curds from the cattle, and milk of the flock,
With fat of lambs; And rams of the breed of Bashan, and goats,
With the choicest wheat; And you drank wine, the blood of the grapes.
15 "But Jeshurun grew fat and kicked;
You grew fat, you grew thick, You are obese!
Then he forsook God who made him,
And scornfully esteemed the Rock of his salvation.
16 They provoked Him to jealousy with foreign gods;
With abominations they provoked Him to anger.
17 They sacrificed to demons, not to God,
To gods they did not know, To new gods,

new arrivals That your fathers did not fear.
18 Of the Rock who begot you, you are unmindful,
And have forgotten the God who fathered you.
19 "And when the LORD saw it, He spurned them,
Because of the provocation of His sons and His daughters.
20 And He said: 'I will hide My face from them,
I will see what their end will be,
For they are a perverse generation,
Children in whom is no faith. 21
They have provoked Me to jealousy by what is not God;
They have moved Me to anger by their foolish idols.
But I will provoke them to jealousy by those who are not a nation;
I will move them to anger by a foolish nation.
22 For a fire is kindled in My anger,
And shall burn to the lowest hell;
It shall consume the earth with her increase,
And set on fire the foundations of the mountains.
23 'I will heap disasters on them; I will spend My arrows on them.
24 They shall be wasted with hunger,
Devoured by pestilence and bitter destruction;
I will also send against them the teeth of beasts,
With the poison of serpents of the dust.
25 The sword shall destroy outside;
There shall be terror within
For the young man and virgin,
The nursing child with the man of gray hairs.
26 I would have said, "I will dash them in pieces,
I will make the memory of them to cease from among men,"
27 Had I not feared the wrath of the enemy,
Lest their adversaries should misunderstand,
Lest they should say," Our hand is high;
And it is not the LORD who has done all this.'"

28 *"For they are a nation void of counsel,*
Nor is there any understanding in them.
29 Oh, that they were wise, that they understood this,
That they would consider their latter end!
30 How could one chase a thousand,
And two put ten thousand to flight,
Unless their Rock had sold them,
And the LORD had surrendered them?
31 For their rock is not like our Rock,
Even our enemies themselves being judges.
32 For their vine is of the vine of Sodom
And of the fields of Gomorrah;
Their grapes are grapes of gall,
Their clusters are bitter.
33 Their wine is the poison of serpents,
And the cruel venom of cobras.
34 'Is this not laid up in store with Me,
Sealed up among My treasures?
35 Vengeance is Mine, and recompense;
Their foot shall slip in due time;
For the day of their calamity is at hand,
And the things to come hasten upon them.'
36 "For the LORD will judge His people
And have compassion on His servants,
When He sees that their power is gone,
And there is no one remaining, bond or free.
37 He will say: 'Where are their gods,
The rock in which they sought refuge?
38 Who ate the fat of their sacrifices,
And drank the wine of their drink offering?
Let them rise and help you, And be your refuge.
39 'Now see that I, even I, am He, And there is no God besides Me;

I kill and I make alive; I wound and I heal;
Nor is there any who can deliver from My hand.
40 For I raise My hand to heaven,
And say, "As I live forever,
41 If I whet My glittering sword, And My hand takes hold on judgment,
I will render vengeance to My enemies, And repay those who hate Me.
42 I will make My arrows drunk with blood,
And My sword shall devour flesh,
With the blood of the slain and the captives,
From the heads of the leaders of the enemy."'
43 "Rejoice, O Gentiles, with His people;
For He will avenge the blood of His servants,
And render vengeance to His adversaries;
He will provide atonement for His land and His people."

Chapter 15
Promises

Thursday afternoon was clear but cold. After Becca had fixed the twins a snack, they went to their room to play video games. The kitchen smelled good, because Becca's mom had put on a pot of beans to slow-cook all day. Becca and Grandma were at the kitchen table preparing to read some of the scriptures which Brother Owens had assigned when they heard the doorbell ring. Answering the door, Becca was surprised to find Mike and Jenny. Becca looked first at Jenny, then at Mike, and then back at Jenny. Even though Mike was smiling, Jenny appeared to be upset and nervous.

"Hi, Jenny," Becca said, "It is good to see you. Please come in."

Mike gave Jenny a nudge of encouragement as both of them stepped into the house. Becca looked to Mike for a clue, wondering under what conditions Jenny was here.

"Grandma and I are in the kitchen. Would you like to join us? We have some drinks and cake." Becca smiled at both Mike and Jenny.

"I'll join Grandma in the kitchen," offered Mike. "I think you and Jenny need to talk in private." As Mike slipped into the kitchen, Becca and Jenny turned into the living room. They sat on the sofa, but at first neither girl spoke. Becca saw a tear trickling down Jenny's cheek.

"Oh, Jenny, please don't cry," said Becca with tears starting to well up in her own eyes. "It's just that you're my very best friend and I don't want to lose you."

Jenny then looked at Becca and noticed the tears on Becca's face. As both girls began wiping tears, they began to laugh. They had often laughed at each other in the past for crying over movies, sentimental commercials, and greeting cards. Both had tender hearts.

Becca started to speak, but Jenny held up her hand to stop her. Clearing her throat, Jenny said, "Becca, I'm sorry I have been giving you the cold shoulder. We have been friends for a long time and it was wrong of me to treat you that way; but my dad really scared me. This uproar about Brother Owens consumes all of my dad's spare time. He is always talking – or I should say, shouting about it –with my Mom or with anyone who will listen, either in person or on the phone. He is really upset. I knew that he was upset about something that Saturday I came over here. Remember, you were asking about your grandpa and what happens after death. When I went home that day, I asked my mom about your question. She immediately told Dad, and he jumped to the conclusion that your family agrees with Brother Owens. He got so angry that he said I wasn't to see you or talk to you anymore. He more or less said you were going to hell if you believed this heresy and that he didn't want me to listen to one word of it."

When Jenny paused, Becca questioned, "So why are you here?"

"Well, Mike came to see me and he said some things that made sense. He said he thought we could still be friends if we would just agree not to discuss that topic. However, he also pointed out that I am old enough to make up my own mind. Instead of studying the Bible with you, I could study on my own, but I am not sure I will understand without help. I'm not really sure what has everyone so upset."

Hoping to make peace, Becca suggested, "I don't want you to be in trouble with your dad, so maybe you shouldn't come over here or call me; but surely we could eat together at school and, yes, agree not to talk about the Bible, church or anything related to Brother Owens – at least for the time being."

Jenny smiled and said, "OK, good."

Becca added one more stipulation, "Jenny, promise me that whenever there is a problem between us, we will talk about it and tell each other the truth. Will you promise me that?" asked Becca.

"Yes, I promise," answered Jenny. The girls hugged each other before joining Grandma and Mike.

Entering the kitchen, Jenny greeted Grandma. Mike and Grandma were snacking on last night's cake. Grandma offered Jenny a serving, entreating, "Sit down with us and have a piece of cake."

"No, I really must go, but thank you," said Jenny.

Becca and Mike exchanged looks. Becca's smile told him that everything was better. Mike quickly scooped the last two bites of cake into his mouth and rose to take Jenny home. As he turned to Grandma, saying, "Thanks for the cake and the visit, Mrs. Elliott," Becca caught him giving a wink to her grandma.

"Son, you don't have to call me 'Mrs. Elliott'. Please call me Grandma as everyone else does."

The moment Mike and Jenny left, Becca inquired, "OK, Grandma. Why did Mike wink at you? Just what were you two visiting about?"

"Wink? What wink?" asked Grandma. "I didn't see a wink. I don't know what you are talking about. Oh, and by the way, if I haven't mentioned it, I like that young man."

"Yeah, I like him, too," agreed Becca. "Shall we start reading?"

"Are things okay between you and Jenny?" asked Grandma.

"Things are better," said Becca, "but not perfect. She can't come over here or call, but we've agreed to be friends at school. Her dad is really upset. He thinks that what Brother Owens is teaching is heresy, so Jenny and I have decided not to discuss Bible issues until this is settled."

"Yes," said Grandma, "I'm sure he does think it is heresy, but I wonder how much he has actually studied this issue from the Bible itself."

"Do you know what has him so upset?" asked Becca.

"I'm sure it's the same question we are studying – whether or not the Second Coming of Christ was in 70 A.D. Is the Second Coming of Christ a literal, bodily coming with physical bodies being resurrected? Or could it be a spiritual coming with believers being raised into a covenant relationship with God?"

Becca took a deep breath and stated, "We had better get some studying done ourselves."

Grandma apologized, "I'm sorry, Becca, but I think I need to return to my bed. You can read to me while I am lying down."

When Grandma was back in bed, Becca began, "Our first scripture is Isaiah 25:6-9." Becca read the following:

> *Isa. 25:6 And in this mountain The LORD of hosts will make for all people A feast of choice pieces, A feast of wines on the lees, Of fat things full of marrow, Of well-refined wines on the lees. 7 And He will destroy on this mountain, The surface of the covering cast over all people, And the veil that is spread over all nations. 8 He will swallow up death forever, And the Lord GOD will wipe away tears from all faces; The rebuke of His people He will take away from all the earth; For the LORD has spoken. 9 And it will be said in that day: "Behold, this is our God; We have waited for Him, and He will save us. This is the LORD; We have waited for Him; We will be glad and rejoice in His salvation."*

"What do you hear the prophet saying?" queried Grandma.

Becca began, "That the Lord will make a feast for all people, and that is good. He will also destroy something and I think that the something may be *death*. That would be good, too. And here is a phrase that we have always associated with heaven – '*no tears*'. This passage ends by saying that the people have waited for God to save them."

Grandma added, "Deliverance from death is salvation. Would it be fair to say that when this happens it would fulfill the prophecy made to Abraham – that through his descendants all people would be blessed? '*The Lord of hosts will make for all people a feast…*'."

"But," asked Becca, "has death really been destroyed?"

Grandma smiled and replied, "That depends on what kind of death it is talking about, doesn't it?"

"Oh, yeah," said Becca. "I keep forgetting about spiritual death. Christ has offered a way to escape spiritual death. He has offered salvation. Do we have salvation now or do we receive it after our physical life is over if we have lived faithfully?"

"What did baptism do for you?" reminded Grandma.

"Washed away my sins?" suggested Becca.

"That is destroying the cause of spiritual death, isn't it?" answered Grandma. "Do you continue to cry and seek a solution for sin?"

"No tears," answered Becca. "Christ has paid the debt."

"Isn't salvation wonderful? Let's try the next passage, Isaiah 26:19-21," said Grandma.

> *Isa 26:19 Your dead shall live;*
> *Together with my dead body they shall arise.*
> *Awake and sing, you who dwell in dust;*
> *For your dew is like the dew of herbs,*
> *And the earth shall cast out the dead.*

Becca read the passage aloud and said to Grandma, "You take this one."

Grandma said, "This passage is talking about Resurrection; but let's remember that our purpose is to determine if Resurrection was promised to Israel. In this scripture, Isaiah is prophesying to Israel. He is telling them that when the Messiah is resurrected, they will be resurrected, also. Yes, I think this promise is to Israel."

"Oh, yes," said Becca. "I would say Resurrection was promised to Israel."

Grandma continued, "I want to ask Brother Owens about the Resurrection of the physically dead. I think their souls were brought out of the land of the dead and assigned to their eternal fate, whereas the physically alive would be spiritually raised into Life in Christ through baptism. I want to ask his opinion on this matter. What passage is next?"

> *Isa. 66:5 Hear the word of the LORD, You who tremble at His word: "Your brethren who hated you, Who cast you out for My name's sake, said, Let the LORD be glorified, That we may see your joy. 'But they shall be ashamed.'"*
>
> *6 The sound of noise from the city! A voice from the temple! The voice of the LORD, Who fully repays His enemies!*
>
> *7 "Before she was in labor, she gave birth; Before her pain came, She delivered a male child. 8 Who has heard such a thing? Who has seen such things? Shall the earth be made to give birth in one day? Or shall a nation be born at once? For as soon as Zion was in labor, She gave birth to her children. 9 Shall I bring to the time of birth, and not cause delivery?" says the LORD. "Shall I who cause delivery shut up the womb?" says your God. 10 "Rejoice with Jerusalem, And be glad with her, all you who love her; Rejoice for joy with her, all you who mourn for her;*
>
> *11 That you may feed and be satisfied With the consolation of her bosom, that you may drink deeply and be delighted With the abundance of her glory."*
>
> *12 For thus says the LORD:*

"Behold, I will extend peace to her like a river, And the glory of the Gentiles like a flowing stream. Then you shall feed; On her sides shall you be carried, And be dandled on her knees. 13 As one whom his mother comforts, So I will comfort you; And you shall be comforted in Jerusalem."

14 When you see this, your heart shall rejoice, And your bones shall flourish like grass; The hand of the LORD shall be known to His servants, And His indignation to His enemies. 15 For behold, the LORD will come with fire And with His chariots, like a whirlwind, To render His anger with fury, And His rebuke with flames of fire. 16 For by fire and by His sword The LORD will judge all flesh; And the slain of the LORD shall be many.

17 "Those who sanctify themselves and purify themselves, To go to the gardens After an idol in the midst, Eating swine's flesh and the abomination and the mouse, Shall be consumed together," says the LORD.

After reading the passage, Becca volunteered, "There is a lot of imagery here, but I think I understand. The Christ will be born through Israel just as God had promised, and He will bring not only Salvation and Joy but Judgment and Destruction, also. In verse 12, the Gentiles are included, and in verse 14, I see an allusion to Resurrection. Finally, verse 16 is about Judgment."

"You are doing very well," said Grandma.

Becca continued. "And it also seems to me that all these things – the bringing of Salvation, Resurrection and Judgment – will happen at the same time, not for Israel alone, but rather for all people."

"The next passage is Ezekiel 37," said Becca.

"I'm sorry you have to do all the reading, Dear," said Grandma.

"Oh, that is all right," said Becca as she began to read.

Ezek 37:1 The hand of the LORD came upon me and brought me out in the Spirit of the LORD, and set me down in the midst of the valley; and it was full of bones. 2 Then He caused me to pass by them all around, and behold, there were very many in the open valley; and indeed they were very dry. 3 And He said to me, "Son of man, can these bones live?"

So I answered, "O Lord GOD, You know."

4 Again He said to me, "Prophesy to these bones, and say to them, 'O dry bones, hear the word of the LORD! 5 Thus says the Lord GOD to these bones: "Surely I will cause breath to enter into you, and you shall live. 6 I will put sinews on you and bring flesh upon you, cover you with skin and put breath in you; and you shall live. Then you shall know that I am the LORD."'"

7 So I prophesied as I was commanded; and as I prophesied, there was a noise, and suddenly a rattling; and the bones came together, bone to bone. 8 Indeed, as I looked, the sinews and the flesh came upon them, and the skin covered them over; but there was no breath in them.

9 Also He said to me, "Prophesy to the breath, prophesy, son of man, and say to the breath, 'Thus says the Lord GOD: "Come from the four winds, O breath, and breathe on these slain, that they may live."'" 10 So I prophesied as He commanded me, and breath came into them, and they lived, and stood upon their feet, an exceedingly great army.

11 Then He said to me, "Son of man, these bones are the whole house of Israel. They indeed say, 'Our bones are dry, our hope is lost, and we ourselves are cut off!' 12 Therefore prophesy and say to them, 'Thus says the Lord GOD: "Behold, O My people, I will open your graves and cause you to come up from your graves, and bring you into the land of Israel. 13 Then you shall know that I am the LORD, when I have opened your graves, O My people, and brought you up from your graves. 14 I will put My Spirit in you, and you shall live, and I will place you in your own land. Then you shall know that I, the LORD, have spoken it and performed it," says the LORD.'"

15 Again the word of the LORD came to me, saying, 16 "As for you, son of man, take a stick for yourself and write on it: 'For Judah and for the children of Israel, his companions.' Then take another stick and write on it, 'For Joseph, the stick of Ephraim, and for all the house of Israel, his companions.' 17 Then join them one to another for yourself into one stick, and they will become one in your hand.

18 "And when the children of your people speak to you, saying, 'Will you not show us what you mean by these?' — 19 say to them, 'Thus says the Lord GOD: "Surely I will take the stick of Joseph, which is in the hand of Ephraim, and the tribes of Israel, his companions; and I will join them with it, with the stick of Judah, and make them one stick, and they will be one in My hand."' 20 And the sticks on which you write will be in your hand before their eyes.

21 "Then say to them, 'Thus says the Lord GOD: "Surely I will take the children of Israel from among the nations, wherever they have gone, and will gather them from every side and bring them into their own land; 22 and I will make them one nation in the land, on the mountains of Israel; and one king shall be king over them all; they shall no longer be two nations, nor shall they ever be divided into two kingdoms again. 23 They shall not defile themselves anymore with their idols, nor with their detestable things, nor with any of their transgressions; but I will deliver them from all their dwelling places in which they have sinned, and will cleanse them. Then they shall be My people, and I will be their God.

24 "David My servant shall be king over them, and they shall all have one shepherd; they shall also walk in My judgments and observe My statutes, and do them. 25 Then they shall dwell in the land that I have given to Jacob My servant, where your fathers dwelt; and they shall dwell there, they, their children, and their children's children, forever; and My servant David shall be their prince forever. 26 Moreover I will make a covenant of peace with them, and it shall be an everlasting covenant with them; I will establish them and multiply them, and I will set My sanctuary in their midst forevermore. 27 My tabernacle also shall be with them; indeed I will be their God, and they shall be My people. 28 The nations also will know that I, the LORD, sanctify Israel, when My sanctuary is in their midst forevermore.""

"Oh, I definitely see the Resurrection theme in this reading, and it is stated clearly that the prophet is talking about Israel and Judah," said Becca. "Also, verse 26 mentions a New Covenant – an everlasting covenant. I think David represents Christ, because Jesus was from the lineage of David. And the Lord will dwell with His people forever. But what are the two sticks?"

"Remember," said Grandma, "how Brother Owens explained that Israel split into two kingdoms. The ten northern tribes are called the *lost tribes* because they intermarried with Gentiles and spread out through the world. However, because the salvation that Christ brings with the New Covenant is for all people, those lost tribes receive the same blessings as Judah. Israel and Judah are the two sticks that will be brought back together in Christ. There is a problem here though. Verse 25 says that they will dwell in the *land of Jacob*. So does that mean geographical Canaan, The Promised Land, or is the language figurative, meaning a spiritual land? I want to ask Brother Owens about that."

Becca began the next reading.

Hos. 13 When Ephraim spoke, trembling, He exalted himself in Israel; But when he offended through Baal worship, he died. 2 Now they sin more and more, And have made for themselves molded images, Idols of their silver, according to their skill; All of it is the work of craftsmen. They say of them, "Let the men who sacrifice kiss the calves!" 3 Therefore they shall be like the morning cloud And like the early dew that passes away, Like chaff blown off from a threshing floor And like smoke from a chimney.

4 "Yet I am the LORD your God Ever since the land of Egypt, And you shall know no God but Me; For there is no savior besides Me. 5 I knew you in the wilderness, In the land of great drought. 6 When they had pasture, they were filled; They were filled and their heart was exalted; Therefore they forgot Me.

7 "So I will be to them like a lion; Like a leopard by the road I will lurk; 8 I will meet them like a bear deprived of her cubs; I will tear open their rib cage, And there I will devour them like a lion. The wild beast shall tear them.

9 "O Israel, you are destroyed, But your help is from Me. 10 I will be your King; Where is any other, That he may save you in all your cities? And your judges to whom you said,' Give me a king and princes'? 11 I gave you a king in My anger, And took him away in My wrath.

12 "The iniquity of Ephraim is bound up; His sin is stored up. 13 The sorrows of a woman in childbirth shall come upon him. He is an unwise son, For he should not stay long where children are born.

14 "I will ransom them from the power of the grave; I will redeem them from death. O Death, I will be your plagues! O Grave, I will be your destruction! Pity is hidden from My eyes."

15 Though he is fruitful among his brethren, An east wind shall come; The wind of the LORD shall come up from the wilderness.

Then his spring shall become dry, And his fountain shall be dried up. He shall plunder the treasury of every desirable prize. 16 Samaria is held guilty, For she has rebelled against her God. They shall fall by the sword, Their infants shall be dashed in pieces, And their women with child ripped open.

After Becca had read, she said, "Boy, this is really graphic writing, too gross for me!" said Becca.

"Yes, it is very vivid," said Grandma. "I think God is really trying to tell them how serious this situation is – life and death serious. Let's try to concentrate on the spiritual message. What do you see here?"

"In this passage," said Becca, "I can see that the Coming of Christ can be received in two different ways. He will come with Judgment, both as a Destroyer of the wicked and as a Savior to the faithful. Resurrection is in verse 14. I see that the Coming of the Lord, along with Resurrection and Judgment, was promised to Israel.

"Yes, I agree with you," said Grandma. "Now, let's read the last passage and then it will be time for you to set the table for supper. Frank and Beth will be home soon." Becca remembered the boys and ran to remind them to get busy on their homework. They gave her the ugly face and she promptly returned it.

Seated again with Grandma, Becca turned to Daniel 12 and read:

Dan 12 "At that time Michael shall stand up, The great prince who stands watch over the sons of your people; And there shall be a time of trouble, Such as never was since there was a nation, Even to that time. And at that time your people shall be delivered, Every one who is found written in the book. 2 And many of those who sleep in the dust of the earth shall awake, Some to everlasting life, Some to shame and everlasting contempt. 3 Those who are wise shall shine Like the brightness of the firmament, And those who turn many to righteousness Like the stars forever and ever.

4 "But you, Daniel, shut up the words, and seal the book until the time of the end; many shall run to and fro, and knowledge shall increase."

5 Then I, Daniel, looked; and there stood two others, one on this riverbank and the other on that riverbank. 6 And one said to the man clothed in linen, who was above the waters of the river, "How long shall the fulfillment of these wonders be?"

7 Then I heard the man clothed in linen, who was above the waters of the river, when he held up his right hand and his left hand to heaven, and swore by Him who lives forever, that it shall be for a time, times, and half a time; and when the power of the holy people has been completely shattered, all these things shall be finished.

8 Although I heard, I did not understand. Then I said, "My lord, what shall be the end of these things?"

9 And he said, "Go your way, Daniel, for the words are closed up and sealed till the time of the end. 10 Many shall be purified, made white, and refined, but the wicked shall do wickedly; and none of the wicked shall understand, but the wise shall understand.

11 "And from the time that the daily sacrifice is taken away, and the abomination of desolation is set up, there shall be one thousand two hundred and ninety days. 12 Blessed is he who waits, and comes to the one thousand three hundred and thirty-five days.

13 "But you, go your way till the end; for you shall rest, and will arise to your inheritance at the end of the days."

"Wow, I didn't realize that the Old Testament actually revealed when Christ would come. These are the same things that Christ was talking about in Matthew 24. It mentions the *abomination of desolation*. Oh, yes, I remember that Matthew 24 said '*the abomination of desolation spoken of by Daniel'*. Here it is; this is it! Verse two is talking about Resurrection. Verse seven says, *'when the power of the holy people is completely shattered, all these things shall be finished'*. Wow, Grandma, by the time that Jerusalem is destroyed in 70 A.D. *'all these things shall be finished'*. Christ will have come! The Resurrection of Israel will be finished! Judgment will be finished! The Old will have passed away and the New will be established. Why didn't we see this before?"

"Well, for one thing," began Grandma, "we didn't study it. We thought the Old Testament was for Israel and the New Testament for Christians. We were taught that God was through with Israel at the cross. We tried hard to make every scripture fit our scenario instead of making the scenario fit the scripture. And now, I'm afraid many people won't consider a different scenario or admit that they are wrong. Instead of being reassured by the fact that God kept His promise to Israel, they feel left out that the Coming of the Lord and the Resurrection are not still promises for their future."

Excited by her new understanding, Becca quickly added, "But they *are* for them. When believers are baptized into Christ, they, too, are Resurrected. They are raised into the New Covenant, so they are in covenant relationship with God. There is no scary Judgment in the future in which you must answer for every deed. Christ has washed the record clean. The Judgment is this: if you are in Christ, you're saved – redeemed – no more spiritual death. So, what happens when you die physically?"

"Well," said Grandma, "I think that you pass over into the spirit world and continue to live with God. I feel certain that is where Grandpa is now. Even though he didn't understand when and why everything happened, Jesus was still his Lord and Savior."

"That's really beautiful," said Becca with a quiet smile.

* * *

Soon after Mom and Dad arrived, the family gathered around the kitchen table, except Grandma, who remained in bed. Becca was still beaming from the enlightening study she and Grandma had enjoyed that afternoon. Noticing her mood, Dad remarked, "Well, Becca, I can see that you are quite happy. Has something special happened?"

"Two things, actually," said Becca. "Jenny and I came to an agreement this afternoon. Her dad forbids her to study the Bible with us, but we have decided to have lunch together at school. And the other thing is that, after studying with Grandma, I am really beginning to see where the Resurrection and the Judgment belong in God's plan. Resurrection was promised to Israel, but we can participate in it, too. God has extended the invitation to all people. Those who accept Christ are resurrected in baptism and become participants in the New Covenant."

Dad saw the concern on Beth's face and interjected, "Becca, why don't you allow your mom and me to read the passages for ourselves. After that, we can compare notes. Beth and I will have some time to read tonight. Now, let's enjoy this supper. Becca, these beans taste really good."

"Dad," chided Becca, "you know good and well that Mom made the beans, and, yes, this supper is very good. Thanks, Mom."

Dad continued, "And who made this delicious cornbread?"

"Yes, I made the cornbread," conceded Becca. "I'm glad you like it."

Supper continued with lively family conversation. Dad spent time trying to engage the twins with questions about school and about what was going on behind the garage. Finally, the dishes were cleared away and the kitchen cleaned. Becca said 'goodnight' to everyone and retired upstairs to her room.

She reflected on how much she had enjoyed the day. As she gently brushed her hair at her window, she could see no stars, only swift clouds sailing past the moon. She rejoiced that she and Jenny would be having lunch together at school. Then she remembered Mike and was grateful that he had talked Jenny into coming over for the reconciliation.

Becca suddenly dropped her brush on the bed as she hurried downstairs to call Mike. Passing the kitchen, she noted that Mom and Dad were reading their Bibles at the table. When she dialed Mike's number, his mother picked up on the other end.

"Hello, Mrs. Gibbons. This is Becca Elliott. May I speak with Mike, please?"

"Oh, yes, Becca. I will get him," responded Mike's mom.

A moment later, Mike said brightly, "Hi, Becca."

"Hi, Mike," began Becca. "I called to tell you 'thank you'. Thank you so much for bringing Jenny over today."

"You're welcome," answered Mike. "I'm glad I could help. I was just about to call you, too."

"What about?" asked Becca.

"Does it have to be about anything? Can't I just call to talk?" teased Mike.

"Of course you may. Call anytime," answered Becca.

"OK, I'll do that and you can call anytime, too, you know – just to talk. But, yes, I have a reason to call this time. Mom and Dad would like to invite you to come to dinner with us Saturday night. We are going to The Road House for dinner to celebrate my mom's birthday. My parents suggested I ask you to join us. Will you come?"

"Yes, I would love to. Thank them for including me," responded Becca.

"Good. I think we will dress up, you know, to make it special for Mom," included Mike.

"OK," said Becca. "Mike, have you had a chance to read the passages Brother Owens suggested?"

"No, not yet," answered Mike.

"Well, when you do, I would like to hear what you think about them," said Becca. "Did your Mom and Dad agree to listen to the recording of last night's lesson?"

"No, I haven't had a chance to mention it yet," answered Mike.

"My mom and dad are reading the next assignment in the kitchen right now," said Becca.

"Well, right now will be as good a time as any to talk to mine," said Mike. "So I'll say goodnight to you and go try."

"Goodnight, Mike," said Becca. "And thank you again for helping Jenny and me to get back together."

"No problem," answered Mike. "Goodnight."

Becca returned to gaze out her window. "Thank you, God, for all the wonderful people in my life. Thank you for the gift of your Son. Thank you for the Bible, which tells us of your Plan of Salvation. Thank you, God, for including all people in the opportunity to have salvation. In Jesus' Name, Amen."

Chapter 16
The Birthday Celebration

On Saturday afternoon, Becca began preparing for Mrs. Gibbons' birthday celebration. Becca had purchased a lovely picture frame to give to Mrs. Gibbons. She wrapped it in silver paper with gold and silver ribbons tied in a double bow. Becca's mom assured her that Mrs. Gibbons would love it.

Becca usually wore her medium length brown hair tied up in a bouncy pony tail. However, by two o'clock in the afternoon, she sat with her hair in rollers while polishing her fingernails with a pale pink polish. She had decided to wear a navy blue wool dress that was belted at the waist. Because the dress had a plain neckline, she planned to wear a necklace to dress it up a bit.

The early afternoon seemed to drag by; then, all of a sudden, it was time to get ready. Mike had said that they would come by for her between six and six-thirty. Because Becca did not want to keep Mike's parents waiting, she was ready promptly at six o'clock. When she came downstairs, the twins gave her the ugly face before vanishing to their room; but, she could see by the way their eyes lit-up that they were impressed. Of course, Dad made a big to-do over her. He whistled at her as he had her turn around. The smiles on Mom's and Grandma's faces showed how proud they were of her, too.

Becca noticed Grandma and Mom whispering with each other as they left the room. When they returned, Grandma was carrying her string of pearls. Grandma spoke first, "Becca, my father gave me this necklace when I was preparing to marry your grandpa. I, of course, wore it on my wedding day. I loaned it to your mother to wear on her wedding day and I have already decided to leave it to your mother in my will." Grandma looked to Beth to continue.

"As the future caretaker of this family treasure, I would like to loan it to you if you would like to wear it tonight." Beth's eyes shown with amazement.

Becca was overwhelmed. "Oh, thank you, Grandma. Thank you, Mother. It is so beautiful." Beth fastened the string of pearls around Becca's neck. The effect was stunning. Becca felt like royalty. Dad insisted on taking pictures. Mom took a picture of Becca with Dad and Dad took a picture of Becca with Mom and then one of Becca with Grandma.

When the doorbell rang, Dad motioned to Becca that he would open the door. In a moment, Mike stepped into the living room with Dad. Becca had never seen Mike wear a suit to church; but, there he stood in a suit and with a corsage in his hand. Becca's heart melted. Becca saw Mike's eyes light up when he saw her. He stepped across the room to her and softly whispered, "You look beautiful."

Mom helped Mike attach the corsage and then, of course, Dad took a picture of Becca and Mike together. After saying goodbye to Becca's parents, they were on their way. Becca was surprised when Mike guided her to the front seat of the car; and, as she was getting in, she saw Mike's mom and dad in the back seat.

"Good evening," said Becca to Mr. and Mrs. Gibbons. "Happy birthday, Mrs. Gibbons."

Mike's mom answered, "Good evening, Becca. I am so glad you could join us."

"Thank you for inviting me," returned Becca.

As Mike got into the driver's seat, he said, "I'm the chauffer tonight. Is every one buckled-up?"

* * *

Once they were seated at the restaurant and the selections from the menu were finished, the conversation began with general questions about school and future plans.

After a few minutes, Mr. Gibbons asked, "What's your opinion of our new preacher, Becca?"

Becca saw Mike quickly look at her, but she couldn't read his expression. Turning back to Mr. Gibbons, she said, "I think he is an excellent preacher. I have learned more about the Bible from his teaching then any preacher I have ever heard. He is very encouraging, and I really enjoyed his lesson on grace last Sunday."

Mike's dad continued, "Yes, that was a good sermon, but every once in while his teaching certainly departs from our tradition."

Becca did not respond and was happy to see that their food had arrived. However, after everyone had begun to eat, Mr. Gibbons returned to the topic, "Well, Becca, we know that your family and Mike have been studying some issues that involve the Second Coming of Christ. What have you found out so far?"

Becca began thoughtfully, "There are a couple of scriptures like Matthew 24:34 and Mathew 5:17-18 that have caused us to search for some answers. Mr. Gibbons, do you think that the Resurrection and Judgment were promises made to Old Covenant Israel or to the church?" After asking the question, Becca was a little sorry that she had put Mr. Gibbons on the spot, but he had put her on the spot first.

Before Mr. Gibbons could answer, Mike inserted, "I am finding the study with Brother Owens very interesting. Like I asked you the other night, Dad, I wish you and Mom would listen to the tape of our last study; and I'm sure you would be welcome to join our study group."

Becca jumped in, "Oh, yes, that would be great. We study on Tuesday evenings."

Mike's mom looked concerned and said, "Oh, I don't know."

Mr. Gibbons responded, "We'll consider it."

Thankfully, Mike changed the subject, "Well, I think it's time for the birthday girl's presents." From an inside pocket of his jacket, Mike pulled a small box and passed it to his mom.

When the box was opened, Mrs. Gibbons exclaimed, "Oh, Mike, how beautiful." Mike had given his mother a delicate bracelet with a diamond pendant. Becca reached under her chair for her gift to Mrs. Gibbons and passed it across the table.

"Oh, Becca," said Mrs. Gibbons, "aren't you sweet?" The picture frame was a success.

Last of all, Mr. Gibbons presented his gift to her. He leaned toward her and they kissed. Mrs. Gibbons said, "And what have you here?" She opened the box to reveal diamond earrings. "Oh, John, they are beautiful. Thank you. Thank you all. This has been a lovely birthday."

As if on cue, the restaurant staff gathered around their table, sang a crazy version of *Happy Birthday* to Mrs. Gibbons, and placed a small birthday cake in front of her. She thought a moment before blowing out the candle as everyone clapped. Becca was glad that Mrs. Gibbons was enjoying her birthday.

As they were walking to the car, Mr. Gibbons said something that Becca really appreciated, "You know, kids, when I heard what topic you are studying, it shocked me. I wondered how could there be any doubt that the Resurrection isn't still future. But, like your parents, Becca, I have been in Brother Owens' Sunday morning class. I must admit that Brother Owens has some interesting points on scriptural concepts we have not studied before. So, while I am not sure about the Second Coming issue, I am sure about this: I don't want this issue to split this congregation as it did the congregation at Cedarville. That's what I am worried about."

"Why do congregations split over things they don't agree on?" asked Mike.

"Well, son, I guess it is because some folks think it is an issue of doctrine. If they believe the doctrine is truth, then they assume anyone who doesn't believe it must be lost. However, to the ones who don't believe it, it is considered heresy. You must admit that in this case that there is a pretty big difference between whether the Second Coming of Christ is past or future. How does this affect other doctrines?"

"My grandma said something like that," said Becca. "She said it is connected to our understanding of a lot of issues." After they were in the car, Becca turned to Mr. and Mrs. Gibbons to invite them once more. "Please listen to the tape Mike made for you and join us next Tuesday night. Mike can give you the list of scriptures we have already studied. I hope you aren't afraid of homework." Everyone laughed.

"We'll consider it. I do appreciate that there are serious young people like you and Mike who care enough to study the Bible."

When they arrived at the Gibbon's home, Becca said 'goodnight' as Mike opened the door for his parents to get out. Hugging his mom, Mike said 'Happy Birthday' one more time.

"Well," began Mike as he turned to Becca, "it's still early. What would you like to do?" After checking the time, they decided that it was too late for the movies, and they were not dressed appropriately for star gazing or bowling.

"Would you like to come over to my house?" asked Becca. "We could put a movie in the DVD or play some games at the kitchen table."

"Sure," said Mike with a smile, "sounds great. Since the governor didn't invite us to his fancy dress ball, what are our choices?"

As Mike and Becca entered her home, however, the mood changed abruptly. The twins were sitting at the kitchen table looking frightened, while Becca's mom and dad were conferring in hushed tones at Grandma's door.

"Is something wrong?" Becca asked as she hurried past the twins.

Joe replied, "Grandma fainted."

When Becca's mom noticed her, she said, "Oh, I'm glad you are home, Sweetie. We called the doctor and he urged us to take Grandma to the emergency room immediately. We were just trying to decide who would take her and who would stay with the boys. Now you can stay with the boys, Becca, so that Dad and I can both go."

"What's wrong?" asked Becca.

"Her blood pressure is low," said Mom. "She fainted in the bathroom while getting ready for bed."

"Will she be all right?" asked Becca.

"I'm sure she will, but we are going to take her to the emergency room just to be safe."

Mike helped Frank get Grandma into the backseat of the car. Becca's mom slipped in beside Grandma. As the tail-lights on the car disappeared around the corner, Becca, Mike and twins went back into the house.

Becca checked the clock and stated to the twins, "It's about time for you two to get ready for bed."

Joe was incredulous, "You mean you are going to make us go to bed when we don't even know if Grandma is going to be OK?"

Jim added even more defiantly, "I'm not going to bed!"

Mike came to the boys' rescue, "Maybe it would be all right for Joe and Jim to stay up a little longer – at least till we hear about your grandma's condition." Joe, Jim and Mike all appealed to Becca with pleading eyes.

"Well, OK, a little while longer," conceded Becca.

"What shall we do then?" asked Mike in a more cheerful voice. "Movie, games, what?"

"Hey," suggested Jim to Mike, "do you like video games? We have several good ones."

"Yeah," said Mike, "I love video games, but I suspect that would not be very much fun for Becca."

Both boys gave Becca the ugly face and she promptly gave it back.

"I don't mind," said Becca. "You guys go ahead and play."

Mike looked at Becca with his eyebrows raised, "Are you sure?"

"Sure, I'm sure," said Becca with a smile and then for fun she gave Mike the ugly face. Joe and Jim thought that was hilarious.

Mike looked at the twins with his eyebrows raised and then gave Becca the ugly face. The twins were having a good laugh until Mike leaned forward to give Becca a quick kiss on the lips. He then turned and gave the ugly face to the boys. Joe and Jim erupted in a chorus of, "O, gross, yuck."

Mike and the boys disappeared up the stairs to the boys' bedroom. Becca went to the kitchen and sat at the table. She laid her head down on her arms and silently prayed, "Dear Heavenly Father, please let Grandma be well." After Becca's nerves had calmed a bit, she got up and opened the refrigerator. She got out two Dr. Peppers and poured two glasses of milk. She found a package of Oreos in the cabinet. Then, with all the refreshments on a tray, she went upstairs to the boys' room. Mike had laid his suit coat and tie on the top bunk, pulled out his shirt tail, kicked off his shoes, and was sitting cross-legged in the floor between Joe and Jim. Mike was the only one who said 'thanks' and smiled up at her as she passed out drinks and set the plate of cookies on the floor in front of them. Jim already had a cookie in his mouth as he muttered, "Out of the way, Sis." She had momentarily blocked his view of the screen.

She watched them play for a while before going to her room to change clothes. She carefully laid the pearl necklace on her dresser and hung up her dress. Just as she finished changing into jeans and a sweatshirt, the phone rang below. She flew downstairs to answer the phone as Joe, Jim and Mike appeared from the boys' bedroom.

"Hello," Becca almost yelled into the phone.

"Hi, Sweetie, it's Mom," said Beth.

"How's Grandma?" asked Becca.

"The doctor just finished with her," began Mom. "The nurse gave her some medication and her blood pressure is already coming up. She should be fine."

"Oh, good," said Becca as she smiled and shook her head encouragingly at the boys and Mike.

Mom continued, "The doctor wants her to stay overnight to make sure she's stable, and they may do some tests to determine if her blood pressure medication needs to be adjusted. I want to stay with her, so your dad is coming home to get some things for me. Would you pack a bag for me, Sweetie? I need my creams, makeup and a change of clothes. One pair of jeans and a clean shirt should be enough. Oh, don't forget my toothbrush. Will you pack those for me?"

"Of course, Mom," said Becca. "Mom?"

"Yes, Sweetie," replied Mom.

"Tell Grandma, 'we all love her'," said Becca.

"OK," said Mom, "Goodnight, Sweetie."

"Goodnight, Mom," said Becca. "We love you, too."

Becca relayed to the boys and Mike what Mom had said. She also told the boys they could stay up to see Dad when he came to get Mom's bag. The boys and Mike returned to the video game while Becca packed Mom's bag.

When Becca's dad arrived about fifteen minutes later, he retold basically the same details that Mom had reported. He confirmed it was definitely time for the boys to get to bed. Mike thought the time was right for him to leave, too; but, Becca's dad asked, "Mike, I will probably be gone 30 to 45 minutes to take this bag to Beth and check on Mom one more time. Would you mind staying until I get back?"

"Not at all, Mr. Elliott," answered Mike. "I'll stay."

"Good," said Frank, "I don't want Becca and the boys to be alone this late at night."

With her dad gone and the boys finally in bed, Becca sat with Mike at the kitchen table. Mike stretched his arms across the table and offered his hands to her. She placed her hands in his. He gently stroked the back of her hands with his thumbs.

"Are you OK?" he asked.

"Yes, but I'm glad you are here," said Becca sweetly.

"I'm glad we decided to come to your house after dinner," said Mike. Remembering the dinner with his folks, Mike said, "I'm sorry my dad put you on the spot with his questions about Brother Owens. I thought you did a great job of answering him."

"Really?" asked Becca. "I was afraid I went too far with that question about the Resurrection and Judgment. Thanks for changing the topic to birthday presents."

"Oh, yeah," said Mike, "speaking of presents, Mom really liked that picture frame you gave her."

"Well, that bracelet you gave her was beautiful," returned Becca.

"I'm glad you liked it," said Mike as he reached inside his suit jacket, which was now hanging on the back of his chair, "because this one is for you."

Becca gasped with surprise as Mike gently pushed a box across the table.

"What's this for? Did you get something for me?" asked Becca trying to suppress her smile.

"I saw it while shopping for Mom's gift," said Mike, "and, well, I just had to buy it for you. Open it," he encouraged.

Becca opened the box and there lay a delicate bracelet with a silver heart suspended from the chain. Tears started in Becca's eyes as she picked up the bracelet.

"Oh, Mike, it is beautiful," said Becca fighting back the tears. "I love it. Thank you, but you shouldn't have."

"Couldn't help myself," said Mike. "It just said, 'buy me for Becca'; so, I did."

Becca smiled at Mike, not knowing what to say next. She didn't want to ruin their relationship by jumping the gun and saying something like "I love you' and possibly scaring Mike away. But she felt in her heart that it was possible that she was falling in love with Mike. As she was wondering what Mike was thinking, he began to describe his feelings to her.

"Becca," began Mike, "I'm not one to say something I don't mean. I just thought the bracelet was perfect for you and I wanted you to have it. I know this: I like you a lot. You're beautiful and you're fun to be with. And even more important, you're intelligent and thoughtful." Mike stopped and laughed. "I despise airhead, giggling girls." He rolled his eyes and then on a more serious note said, "Maybe that's the difference, you're more of a woman than a girl."

Becca blushed. She didn't know how to respond, so she simply replied, "Thank you." Extending her arm across the table, she asked, "Can you fasten it for me?"

"Sure," Mike said as he closed the clasp on the bracelet. Mike held both of Becca's hands in the middle of the table. "But," Mike said in a firmer voice, "I don't like being so far away from you! How about meeting me at the end of the table?"

At the end of the table, Becca put her hands around the back of his head, pulled it down and gave him a firm, fun kiss. He laughed, pulled her tighter into his arms and gave her one long, soft, serious kiss and then another.

When he released her, he lightened the mood with a 'wow' and a tiger growl. They both laughed. Still standing in front of him, Becca said, "And do you know what I like about you?"

"No, what?" asked Mike.

Becca said, "You're handsome, polite, nice to my parents and brothers, and you, too, are a very thoughtful person. Yes, I think I like you and, uh, I like your kisses, too."

Mike again pulled her close and they kissed – a long soft gentle kiss. Becca felt warm as she had never felt before. She didn't want the kiss or the embrace to end and she imagined that Mike felt the same way, but the kiss did end and Becca suggested, "Why don't we pick out a movie to watch. Mike chose a movie and they had watched only twenty minutes of it when they heard the car door shut in the driveway.

Once indoors, Dad confirmed that Grandma was doing well. After Mike had gone, Becca stood at her window. "Thank you, Father, for taking care of Grandma. Help her to be well so that she may be with us for many more years. Please open Mike's parents' minds to study with us. And, Father, thank you for Mom, Dad, my brothers and Mike. Bless them all. In Jesus' Name, Amen."

Chapter 17
Brother Owens' Class

Frank was up early the next morning. He woke Becca and said, "Sis, it is six o'clock. I'm going to the hospital to check on Grandma. Your mom or I will be back here by eight o'clock to get everyone up for church."

Becca replied, "OK, Dad," and smiled at him, then turned over and fell back asleep. The next thing she knew, Dad had returned. From downstairs, she heard him call, "Hey, kids, everyone up. Joe! Jim! Becca! Everyone, get up. I brought fresh cinnamon rolls from the bakery."

Becca heard the boys scurrying down the steps as she pulled on her robe and ran down the stairs herself. "Morning, Sis," said Dad as she entered the kitchen.

"Morning. How's Grandma?" Becca asked.

"Doing fine, but the doctor wants to keep her one more day to make sure they have her blood pressure medication right," said Dad. "We'll go to church and then we'll all go to the hospital to visit her. I'm going to stay at the hospital this afternoon and let your mom come home for a nap."

As they drove to church that morning, Becca asked, "Dad, do you think it would be all right if I came to your Sunday school class? I think I would learn more in Brother Owens' class than in the high school class."

"Oh, well, that might furrow some brows, and it might hurt Mr. Simms' feelings, but I'm for it," answered Dad.

"Well, I don't want to hurt Mr. Simms' feelings," said Becca. "Maybe I should talk to him first."

When they got to the church building, Mike was waiting on the front steps. He hurried out to the parking lot when he saw the Elliott's car. As he opened Becca's door, he asked, "How's your grandma doing?"

"She's doing much better, thanks," returned Becca.

In the building, as Becca and Mike went down the hall together, Becca told Mike that she was going to class with her dad after she talked to Mr. Simms. At the classroom door, Becca motioned to Mr. Simms and said softly, "Could I talk to you for a moment, please?" Mr. Simms stepped into the hall with Becca. Becca began, "Mr. Simms, I appreciate how you have been my teacher for four years now, but they are studying some topics in the adult class that I want to learn more about. I'm going to go to the adult class with my dad, but I just wanted to tell you 'thank you' before I went."

Mr. Simms smiled at Becca, remarked that he had enjoyed having Becca in class, and indicated that he understood that Becca was ready for deeper study. As Becca turned and started down the hall, Mike made his mind up quickly and went with her. Becca's dad was waiting outside the adult class room and they all entered together, taking seats next to Mike's parents and nodding good morning to the people around them. Brother Owens was beginning to make welcoming comments to the class when Mrs. Gibbons leaned over Mr. Gibbons and motioned for Becca to lean closer. Mrs. Gibbons whispered, "I was sorry to hear about your grandma. Is she doing all right?"

"Yes, thank you," Becca whispered back.

When Brother Owens asked if anyone had any announcements, Frank informed the class about Grandma. Everyone nodded in concern and then in relief to hear that she was doing all right. Brother Owens asked the class members to bow their heads in prayer. He asked for God's blessing on the sick, calling them by name, and for God's blessing on their study that morning. The official topic in Brother Owens' class was 'Old Testament Prophecies and their New Testament Fulfillments'. They were studying in the book of Isaiah, chapter 66, verse 15. Brother Owens read:

"For behold, the Lord will come with fire and with His chariots, like a whirlwind, to render His anger with fury, and His rebuke with flames of fire. For by fire and by His sword the Lord will judge all flesh. And the slain of the Lord shall be many."

Brother Owens looked at the class. It seemed to be a moment of decision for him.

He began, "Brothers and sisters, we are again at a scripture over which there may be some disagreement; but I ask you to keep an open mind as we consider the scriptures together. This is a prophecy of Judgment – the Judgment of all flesh. To whom was the prophet prophesying? Remember, in verses eight and nine, someone was expecting something – like a woman expects the birth of a child. It's a sure thing that is going to happen when its time is ready. Which people were expecting something and what were they expecting?" No one spoke in the hushed room. Becca looked at her dad and whispered, "Why doesn't someone answer?"

Taking courage, Becca's dad volunteered, "I think this must be Israel and she is expecting the Messiah to come." Several people now nodded in agreement.

Brother Owens continued, "So when the Messiah comes to Israel, will that be a time of Judgment?" No one, not even Dad, answered.

Brother Owens continued, "Let's read on in verses 18 and 19."

"For I know their works and their thoughts. It shall be that I will gather all nations and tongues; and they shall come and see My glory. I will set a sign among them; and those among them who escape I will send to the nations: to Tarshish and Pul and Lud, who draw the bow, and Tubal and Javan, to the coastlands afar off who have not heard My fame nor seen My glory. And they shall declare My glory among the Gentiles.

"This scripture says that the Lord will gather all nations, and the ones who escape destruction will go throughout the world among the Gentiles. After this judgment the world - the physical world - will still be in existence." Brother Owens paused and looked at the class and then continued, "Let's turn to Matthew 24:30-35. Would someone please volunteer to read these verses?"

No one offered to read aloud, but all were reading silently. Becca was startled when Mike spoke up, saying, "I'll read." Mike didn't know the procedure in the class, whether he could sit or if he should stand to read. He stood and read the passage in a strong clear voice.

Then the sign of the Son of Man will appear in heaven, and then all the tribes of the earth will mourn, and they will see the Son of Man coming on the clouds of heaven with power and great glory. And He will send His angels with a great sound of a trumpet, and they will gather together His elect from the four winds, from one end of heaven to the other.

"Now learn this parable from the fig tree: When its branch has already become tender and puts forth leaves, you know that summer is near. So you also, when you see all these things, know that it is near — at the doors! Assuredly, I say to you, this generation will by no means pass away till all these things take place.

When he sat down, he and Becca exchanged brief smiles.

Brother Owens began again, "Thank you, Mike. Class, we have gone over Matthew 24 several times. Jesus is using the same language and context as Isaiah 66 – the gathering and Judgment promised to Israel: Christ said it would be in that generation." He paused. "I appreciate the difficulty you are having. We were all taught that the Second Coming - the coming in Judgment - would be at the end of the Christian age, but it was actually promised to Israel. The people who had lived under the Old Law were Resurrected – that is, brought from the land of the dead, judged, and given their eternal reward. The accounts of the people of the Old Law had to be judged and settled before the Old Law could pass and the New Covenant could replace it. Those people who were alive in that generation, who accepted Christ as the Son of God and were baptized into Christ were also Resurrected – that is, they were raised from a Covenant of Death into the New Covenant of Life.

I Cor. 2:7 Therefore, if anyone is in Christ, he is a new creation; old things have passed away; behold, all things have become new.'

Rom 6:3-4 'Know ye not, that so many of us as were baptized into Jesus Christ were baptized into his death? Therefore we are buried with him by baptism into death: that like as Christ was raised up from the dead by the glory of the Father, even so we also should walk in newness of life.'

Eph 2:4-8, 'But God, who is rich in mercy, because of His great love with which He loved us, even when we were dead in trespasses, made us alive together with Christ (by grace you have been saved), and raised us up together, and made us sit together in the heavenly places in Christ Jesus, that in the ages to come He might show the exceeding riches of His grace in His kindness toward us in Christ Jesus.'

This is a spiritual covenant-ending Judgment, not a judgment involving the dissolving of the physical world."

This was Mike's main concern, so he asked the question which he suspected that the other class members were probably asking in their minds. Mike said, "Brother Owens, this is one of my main questions. The description of the Second Coming sounds catastrophic. How could it have happened in that generation and we not know about it?"

"That's a very good question, Mike," said Brother Owens. "Let's take time to look at the language. Some prophecies of the Second Coming describe Christ coming on a cloud with the sun being darkened, the stars falling, the elements burning with fervent fire and the heavens being rolled up like a scroll. Is that what you are talking about?" asked Brother Owens looking at Mike and Mike nodded 'yes'.

"Class," said Brother Owens, "let me assign some readings. Who will read?"

Becca's dad raised his hand. "OK, Mr. Elliott, would you get Isaiah 19:1-2."

Mr. Gibbons raised his hand. "Good, Mr. Gibbons, please find Ezekiel 32:7-10.

As other hands were raised, Brother Owens assigned Isaiah 13:9-10, Isaiah 13:19-20, Isaiah 34:1-5, and Isaiah 63:1-6.

Brother Owens began, "During the history of Israel, God often allowed other nations to enslave Israel. When Israel did evil, God sent a judgment against her; but he also sent judgments against the nations who troubled Israel. Isaiah 19:1-2 is about God's judgment against Egypt. Mr. Elliott, would you read your passage?" Following Mike's example, Mr. Elliott stood and read.

> Isa 19:1 Behold, the LORD rides on a swift cloud,
> And will come into Egypt;
> The idols of Egypt will totter at His presence,
> And the heart of Egypt will melt in its midst.

158

2 "I will set Egyptians against Egyptians;
Everyone will fight against his brother,
And everyone against his neighbor,
City against city, kingdom against kingdom.

"Class," said Brother Owens, "please consider this: did God actually ride on a physical cloud, or does this vivid language mean that God is the one who brought the judgment?" Brother Owens did not wait for an answer but asked for the reading of Ezekiel 32:7-10. "The description that Mr. Gibbons is going to read is also about the judgment and destruction of Egypt."

Mr. Gibbons rose to read.

Ezek 32:7 When I put out your light,
I will cover the heavens, and make its stars dark;
I will cover the sun with a cloud,
And the moon shall not give her light.
8 All the bright lights of the heavens I will make dark over you,
And bring darkness upon your land,'
Says the Lord GOD.

9'I will also trouble the hearts of many peoples, when I bring your destruction among the nations, into the countries which you have not known. 10 Yes, I will make many peoples astonished at you, and their kings shall be horribly afraid of you when I brandish My sword before them; and they shall tremble every moment, every man for his own life, in the day of your fall.'

Brother Owens continued, "Does the terminology 'the sun darkened' really mean it was dark that day, or does it mean it was a day of destruction - a day of loss? Don't we also use a similar expression when talking about hard times? We say, 'those were dark days in our history'."

Brother Owens asked for each of the next passages to be read: Isaiah 13:9-10 & 19-20.

Isa 13:9 Behold, the day of the LORD comes,
Cruel, with both wrath and fierce anger,
To lay the land desolate;
And He will destroy its sinners from it.
10 For the stars of heaven and their constellations
Will not give their light;
The sun will be darkened in its going forth,
And the moon will not cause its light to shine.

Isa 13:19 And Babylon, the glory of kingdoms,
The beauty of the Chaldeans' pride,
Will be as when God overthrew Sodom and Gomorrah.
20 It will never be inhabited,
Nor will it be settled from generation to generation;
Nor will the Arabian pitch tents there,
Nor will the shepherds make their sheepfolds there.

Brother Owens continued, "These passages are talking about the destruction of Babylon. It's the same idea of dark times of judgment and loss. The brightness of their glory is put out. They are defeated. Who has Isaiah 34:1-5?"

Isa. 34:1 Come near, you nations, to hear; And heed, you people! Let the earth hear, and all that is in it, The world and all things that come forth from it. 2 For the indignation of the LORD is against all nations, And His fury against all their armies; He has utterly destroyed them, He has given them over to the slaughter. 3 Also their slain shall be thrown out; Their stench shall rise from their corpses, And the mountains shall be melted with their blood. 4 All the host of heaven shall be dissolved, And the heavens shall be rolled up like a scroll; All their host shall fall down As the leaf falls from the vine, And as fruit falling from a fig tree.

5 "For My sword shall be bathed in heaven; Indeed it shall come down on Edom, And on the people of My curse, for judgment.

After the reading was completed, Brother Owens said, "Now, that event would have been impossible to miss if it had been literal. Were the heavens really rolled up as a scroll or is this the same imagery describing the powers in high places being removed, defeated? Let's hear the last passage, Isaiah 63:1-6."

Isa. 63:1 Who is this who comes from Edom, With dyed garments from Bozrah, This One who is glorious in His apparel, Traveling in the greatness of His strength? —

"I who speak in righteousness, mighty to save."

2 Why is Your apparel red, And Your garments like one who treads in the winepress?

3 "I have trodden the winepress alone, And from the peoples no one was with Me. For I have trodden them in My anger, And trampled them in My fury; Their blood is sprinkled upon My garments, And I have stained all My robes. 4 For the day of vengeance is in My heart, And the year of My redeemed has come. 5 I looked, but there was no one to help, And I wondered That there was no one to uphold; Therefore My own arm brought salvation for Me; And My own fury, it sustained Me. 6 I have trodden down the peoples in My anger, Made them drunk in My fury, And brought down their strength to the earth."

"Did the Lord actually go to Edom to stomp grapes in the winepress? No, the scripture uses imagery that means that He caused the defeat of the Edomites by using another nation in battle against them."

There was a short pause as Brother Owens looked around at his class. All eyes were on him. Everyone was listening. "When the Messiah came to Israel, he came to judge them. As a nation, they were declared to be evil and unfaithful to God. What nation did God use to bring an end to the nation of Israel and its capital city, Jerusalem?"

A voice from the back of the room said, "Rome."

"That's correct. And when did that happen?" asked Brother Owens.

The same voice said, "70 A.D."

"That's right. Jerusalem, the priesthood, and the Temple were all destroyed at that time. What did that destruction symbolize?"

Becca leaned over to her dad and asked, "Is it all right for me to answer?"

Dad nodded his head.

Becca raised her hand.

Brother Owens saw it and called upon her, "Yes, Becca."

Becca answered Brother Owens, "I think the Destruction of Jerusalem in 70 A.D. is a huge sign that symbolized the destruction of the Heavens and Earth of the Old Covenant that allowed the bringing in of the New Heavens and New Earth of the Messiah."

Brother Owens smiled and shook his head in agreement. "Yes, Becca, I think you are right. Class, I hope you will continue to study these ideas throughout the week. If you have questions, please bring them with you next week." Brother Owens moved away from the podium as the class began to move out of the room. Some small groups stopped to consult with one another as Brother Owens came toward Becca and Mike.

Brother Owens extended his hand to Mike and said, "I'm glad you two decided to join our class today."

Mike answered, "Good morning, sir. Yes, I am glad we came to your class, too."

Brother Owens extended his hand to Mr. Gibbons, "Good Morning, Mr. and Mrs. Gibbons."

Brother Owens turned to Mr. Elliott, "Good morning, Frank. I'm sorry to hear about your mother. I hope she will be all right."

Frank responded, "Thank you. I think she will be fine. She'll be sorry she missed this lesson, but I'll tell her about it."

While Becca, Mike and Frank were talking with Brother Owens, Becca became aware that Mike's dad was standing behind her, listening to their conversation. Mr. Gibbons said, "Frank, Brother Owens, if it is all right with you, I think I would like to join your Tuesday night study."

Becca saw Mike's face. It reflected both pride and pleasure at the same time.

Becca's dad said, "Of course, John. You and Linda are always welcome in our home."

Mrs. Gibbons was not standing with her husband; she had moved over to talk with a group of ladies. Mr. Gibbons replied, "I'll tell Linda that she's invited. I'll be there for sure."

Brother Owens reached across the group and extended his hand to Mr. Gibbons. "I'm glad you will be studying with us," he said.

Mr. Gibbons responded, "I expect that I'm a bit behind. I may need someone to help catch me up on what you have already studied."

"I'll be glad to do that, Dad," said Mike, "although I suspect that Becca is ahead of all of us."

"Becca and her grandma," added Frank as everyone smiled at Becca.

Chapter 18
Conflict

After church services, Frank and the kids went to the hospital to visit Grandma. They discovered Grandma sitting up in bed. She smiled as Becca, Joe and Jim rushed to her side. She said, "I'm sorry, children, I didn't mean to be such a bother."

"Are you OK?" asked Joe.

Grandma replied, "Doctor Green said that I'm doing fine. I just want to go home."

"I'm sure you do, Grandma," said Mom, "but Dr. Green wants to make sure you're not going to be fainting on us again, and besides, not all the results on your blood work are back. I agree with the doctor. You need to stay here at least one more night."

Becca began to tell Grandma and Mom about the morning Bible class. "Brother Owens showed us in the Old Testament the same type of language that the New Testament uses about the Second Coming. I made a note of the scriptures he used." Becca handed Grandma the note. "Maybe you can get Dad to read them to you this afternoon."

Frank said, "Beth, you need some sleep. Let Becca drive you and the boys home. Boys, your mom needs to sleep this afternoon, so you need to remember to be extra quiet. Becca, turn the ringer on the phone down on low."

"When do you want me to come back to relieve you?" asked Beth.

"How about eight o'clock this evening?" suggested Dad. "Mom and I will be fine. We'll have a good visit."

"What about your lunch?" asked Beth.

"Oh, I think Mom will be all right while I go to the cafeteria to get something," answered Frank.

"OK, I guess we'll go now," said Beth. After telling Grandma good-bye, Becca, Joe, Jim and Beth left for home.

At home, Beth ate a bowl of soup before going to bed. Becca fixed sandwiches and chips for herself and her brothers, who soon disappeared into their bedroom. Becca sat at the kitchen table with her school work and her Bible. She had a full schedule planned for the afternoon.

Becca had just finished her homework when the phone rang. As she ran to answer, she looked at her watch. It was four o'clock. "Hello, Elliott's," Becca said.

"Hi," said the voice on the other end, "It's me."

"Hi," said Becca, instantly recognizing Mike's voice.

"How's your Grandma doing?" asked Mike.

"She's much better," answered Becca, "but the doctor wants to keep her until after he checks the lab results of her blood work tomorrow morning."

"Well, things aren't so fine here," said Mike. Becca could tell by the tone in Mike's voice that he was troubled.

"What's wrong?" asked Becca.

"Well, evidently, news about our Tuesday night study with Brother Owens has spread throughout the whole congregation. Even more amazing is how quickly the word spread that my dad was going to join our study. We hadn't finished eating dinner before Jenny's dad, Mr. Phillips, was in our living room with my dad. He asked to speak to Dad privately, but I followed them into the living room. Mr. Phillips looked at me, then at my dad, but since Dad did not ask me to leave, Mr. Phillips said nothing to me."

"Mr. Phillips began by stating that they, meaning Dad and he, had already discussed this matter and had agreed to oppose this teaching. Dad answered that he thought he needed to know more about the teaching before he could be sure which stand to take. Mr. Phillips insisted that he knew about this doctrine and that it would result in splitting a church, and that he didn't want to be a part of anything that would split a church. My dad said that he hoped the church wouldn't split, but that he had to know for himself if the teaching was truth or not. My dad emphasized that truth is always more important than whether everyone agrees or not. Dad said that he thought brotherly love, kindness and patience were called for at this time. My dad also suggested that after he had time to study the topic with Brother Owens that he would be more than glad to study with Mr. Phillips to see if he could accept or refute the conclusion."

"Mr. Phillips looked really exasperated with my dad. He said this doctrine was heresy. He said that anyone with half a brain could see that Christ had not come again. When Mr. Phillips said that, my dad said he had gone too far and asked him to rethink his position. Mr. Phillips must have realized that he had been condescending, because he offered Dad an apology. Dad accepted the apology and again asked Mr. Phillips to be patient."

There was silence for a moment before Becca whispered, "Oh, my goodness, Mike. Mr. Phillips is really upset, isn't he?"

"To say the least, yes," answered Mike.

"I'm really proud of your dad though," said Becca.

"Yeah, me too," said Mike. "Dad did all right. He kept his cool."

"Why are you whispering?" asked Mike.

"Mom's sleeping," said Becca.

"I'll let you go then," said Mike, but he then continued. "Are you going to evening service?"

"Probably not," said Becca. "Mom is going to relieve Dad at the hospital at eight o'clock tonight. So we probably won't go."

"Are you going?" asked Becca.

"Yeah, I think I will," said Mike. "I'll call you later tonight."

"OK," said Becca.

* * *

Becca's mom woke around six o'clock. As they prepared supper, Becca told her mom about Mike's phone call. Mom shook her head sadly and said, "I was afraid something like this would happen. I just don't understand how this doctrine could be truth. How could righteous men and women throughout the years not have discovered this? I just don't understand."

Becca was concerned about her mother's statement. She knew that her mom didn't believe it could be true as they began to study, but she had thought her mom was starting to understand.

"Mom," said Becca.

"Yes, Sweetie," replied her mom.

"I didn't mean to make trouble," said Becca. "I just want to understand what happens to you when you die. I guess understanding this doctrine is not so hard for me, because I didn't have any prior belief about it in the first place."

"Well," said Mom, "I see now that the Resurrection and Judgment were promised to Israel. And I agree that baptism is a Resurrection into a new life. But there are so many scriptures that sound literal that I just don't see how they could all be figurative."

Becca put her arm around her mom's shoulder and said, "Mom, I appreciate that you are studying with us."

"Well," said Beth, looking into Becca's eyes, "I know it would be wrong not to study. I'm sure of that. If you study only the set of scriptures that you think prove your viewpoint, then you won't ever have the complete truth. I believe that all of God's Word has to be in harmony or there would be no way to know the truth."

* * *

Frank and Beth switched places at eight o'clock. Grandma was still feeling well. Frank was taking off from work Monday so that he could visit with the doctor in the morning and bring Grandma home.

At 8:30 the phone rang. Becca hurried to pick it up, hoping to hear Mike's voice.

"Hello, Elliott's," said Becca.

"Hi," said Mike.

"Hi," answered Becca.

"I surely would like to see you," said Mike.

"Dad's home with the boys now," said Becca. "Come over; we can go out for a while if you want to."

"I'll see you in 15 minutes," answered Mike as he hung up the phone.

Becca ran upstairs to check her hair and make-up. She decided to change from her sweatshirt to a sweater. Ten minutes later, as she was descending the stairs, Dad was greeting Mike at the front door. Mike asked Becca if she had told her dad about Mr. Phillips. Becca shook her head 'no', so Mike filled in Mr. Elliott with the details of the exchange between his dad and Mr. Phillips.

"Do you think your dad will still come on Tuesday night?" asked Frank.

"Yes, he will come, but Mom's really upset," said Mike. "I'm pretty sure she won't come."

"That's too bad," responded Frank.

"Well, Mr. Elliott," said Mike, "if you don't mind, I thought I'd take Becca to get a Dr. Pepper."

"Oh, sure," said Dad. "You two go on."

"I won't be late, Dad," said Becca as she and Mike went out the front door.

On the front porch Mike hesitated and said, "Why don't you bring your coat? There is a clear sky tonight and we can do a little star gazing."

Becca ran back in, explaining to Dad that she had forgotten her coat and hurried right back out the front door. Mike was already at the car, holding Becca's door open for her. As soon as she was buckled in, he pulled away.

"Do you want something to drink now or later?" asked Mike.

"Later," said Becca.

Mike drove through the campus to the old campus park. When they arrived at the amphitheater, Becca could see that there were only a few couples there. The two guys with the telescope were not there tonight even though the night was clear. The stars were bright and beautiful. They sat for a long time watching the sky. Mike had his arm around Becca. Suddenly, a bright star streaked across the sky.

Mike asked, "Did you make a wish?"

"Of course," said Becca.

"Well, are you going to tell me what you wished for?" Mike asked.

"No," said Becca matter-of-factly. Then she added, "If I tell you what I wished for, it won't come true."

"Oh, OK, then, what will you tell me?" asked Mike.

Becca turned sideways, sitting so she could see Mike's face. "What do you want to know?" she asked.

"Tell me what you want your life to be like ten years from now," said Mike.

"Ten years from now?" asked Becca. "Wow, I hadn't thought that far ahead." Becca considered for a moment and ventured, "I imagine myself married with, maybe, even a couple of kids by then. First, I want to get a college degree. I just don't know what I want to major in."

"Do you think you will finish college before you get married?" asked Mike.

"Yes, I think so," said Becca, "I think it is wise for a couple to date for at least a year or two to really get to know one another. And then the engagement would probably be for another year. Choosing a mate for life is an important decision."

"Yeah? What will your husband be like?" asked Mike.

"Oh, really handsome, I hope," said Becca. She thought a moment longer and continued. "He will be someone I am really comfortable with, someone I know I can trust with my deepest secrets. He will be intelligent and very dependable. And he will love me just as I am."

"Do you want to work after you have kids?" asked Mike.

"I don't know," said Becca. "If I could find a good sitter it might be OK, because I really do think I want to have a career. I want to make a contribution to life and to my family. I want to know that I could survive on my own if I had to."

Mike was smiling at Becca all the time she was talking about her expectations. Even after she quit talking he continued to smile at her.

"OK, so how do you see your life in ten years?" asked Becca.

"Oh, I want to do safari work and travel around Africa," said Mike.

Becca looked at Mike. His face was as serious as it could be. She was fairly sure he was kidding, so she looked at him just as seriously until he cracked a grin. He reached to pull her close to him. She started to laugh but the laugh was smothered by his kiss. After the kiss Becca continued to sit so that she could see Mike's face.

"How do you see yourself in ten years?" Becca asked again.

"I'm not sure about all the details," said Mike, "but I'm starting to get a pretty good idea."

Becca could see longing and love in Mike's eyes. She really liked Mike and thought she was falling in love with him, but she didn't want their relationship to go too fast. So far, Mike had been very respectful.

Not once had he even tried to go too far with her. Mike had been a perfect gentleman, but right now the look in his eyes scared her a little.

Becca smiled at Mike and said, "I think I'm ready for some hot chocolate. What about you?"

Mike immediately got up, offered his hand to pull her up, and said, "Hot chocolate, it is."

When Becca stood at her window that night, she had a lot to pray for. "Be with Grandma and let her be well. Help Mr. Gibbons and Mr. Phillips to respect each other in Christian love. Guide all of us who want to understand Your Word. Thank you for Mike. In Jesus' Name, Amen."

Chapter 19
Full Moon Agreement

When Becca arrived home from school Monday afternoon, Grandma was sitting in her chair in the bedroom.

"Hi, Grandma," said Becca. "It is so good to have you home. You had us all worried." Becca gave her grandma a quick kiss and sat on the edge of her bed. "Can I get you anything?" asked Becca.

"No, Dear," said Grandma. "I'm fine. Your mother has been doing a good job taking care of me – religiously checking on me every five minutes."

"Did Dad read those scriptures to you that we covered in Sunday morning class?" asked Becca.

"Yes," answered Grandma. "And Beth read them to me again last night. I asked her to read them, even though your dad had already read them to me, because I wanted your mom and me to have a chance to discuss them. We had a really good visit. I think she is starting to see that the Coming of Christ is spiritual – not a literal coming in the physical clouds."

"I'm so glad," said Becca. "Grandma, do you still have questions for Brother Owens – pieces that you don't understand?"

"Yes, I need help understanding the Resurrection and Judgment," said Grandma. "I believe it happened in that generation, but I'm not sure how it all worked. The physically dead were judged; but were the

173

physically alive judged, and was the old system also judged in some manner? I will have to ask him about that."

"Grandma," said Becca. "If the Judgment happened in that generation, are we judged, like, maybe, when we die?"

"That's another good question," said Grandma.

Becca's mom had stepped to Grandma's doorway and said, "Becca, let Grandma rest now. Please help her over to her bed and cover her with that throw. The doctor said she should lie down most of the time. Grandma and I have agreed that for a couple days she will alternately lie down for two hours and sit up for about an half hour. She is scheduled to go for a check-up Thursday morning.

"OK, Mom," said Becca. "Are you ready to stand, Grandma?" Becca helped Grandma to her bed, covered her with the throw, and kissed her on the forehead. "I love you, Grandma," said Becca as she left the room, softly closing the door behind her.

"Is Grandma really all right?" Becca asked Mom in the kitchen.

"The doctor was concerned with the results of her blood work and said that her heart is weak," said Mom. "They drew more blood early this morning to double check the lab results. The doctor wouldn't say more than that. He said to watch her and not to let her walk without help to prevent a fall. Maybe we will learn more on Thursday. Hopefully, her blood work results will be normal."

Becca went up to her room. At first, she lay down on her bed on her back looking at the ceiling, then she turned to her side. There was her window – her own private view of the world. The afternoon sun was hidden behind the clouds. The clouds were thickening and the sky looked as if rain was imminent. A tear ran out of the corner of Becca's eye. She wasn't sure why she was crying. It could certainly be because she was worried about Grandma; but Becca also had a lot of concern on her heart because of the Bible study and the tension it was causing between her and Jenny, between Mom and Dad, between Mr. Gibbons and Mr. Phillips, and between Mike and his parents. Becca was now convinced that Christ had come in the first century. Had she decided too quickly? Were there other scriptures that would cast her new belief into doubt? She felt that she needed to have a good talk with Grandma, but Grandma needed to rest. Becca was afraid she would upset her with all her questions. She also needed to have a good talk with Dad; but, of course, Dad was at work. Maybe later tonight she could talk to him alone.

She was concerned about her relationship with Mike. She wanted a college education and a career to help ensure the probability that she could be self-sufficient.

Yet, she thought she was falling in love with Mike and the Mike she knew thus far was exactly what she wanted as a husband. He was kind and considerate, very good looking, and, most importantly, he was a Christian – a Christian who was interested in knowing God's truth. She wondered if she was what Mike wanted in a girl-friend. What characteristics did he want his wife to have? Was the timing all wrong? Would he want more than she wanted to give at this time? She knew that couples who went too far sexually seldom ended up with a happy relationship. Could their relationship survive years without their becoming sexually involved? Her tears were flowing freely. She did not bother to wipe them away. Falling across her cheeks, the tears had already made a wet circle on her bedspread.

* * *

The next thing Becca became aware of was Mom sitting on the edge of her bed with her hand on Becca's shoulder urging, "Becca, Sweetie, wake up." Becca glanced at the window and saw that it was dark outside. She looked at her mom.

"What time is it?" asked Becca.

"It's six o'clock and dinner is ready," answered Mom. "I thought you were up here doing homework. Are you feeling OK?"

As Becca sat up and rubbed her eyes, she discovered that the corners of her eyes were crusty with dried tears. "I must have fallen asleep," said Becca.

"Were you crying, Sweetie?" asked Mom.

Becca nodded 'yes' as the tears began to flow again.

"What's wrong?" asked Mom. "Are you worried about Grandma?"

Becca nodded her head 'yes', even though Grandma was only part of what was troubling her. She tried to wipe the tears away.

"Grandma's going to be just fine," said Mom. "We'll take good care of her. Won't we?"

Becca managed a small smile, gave her mom a hug and responded, "Yes, of course."

"Why don't you wash your face and come on to eat? We will wait for you if you hurry," said Mom.

"OK," said Becca.

When she entered the kitchen a few minutes later, the family, including Grandma, was all seated at the table. The twins gave Becca the ugly look, but she only smiled in return. They looked disappointed that she hadn't played their ugly face game.

"Hi, Sis. How was school today?" asked Dad.

"It was OK," said Becca, "but I have homework to finish."

"Mom and I need to study the passages for tomorrow night with Brother Owens," said Dad.

"There is a lot to read – sometimes whole chapters," said Becca. "I was really surprised by the chapter in Daniel. It sounded as if it was giving a timeline as to when Christ would come. Did you know about it?" asked Becca.

"Yes, I did, but I don't fully understand it," said Dad. "I'll bet Brother Owens can help us with it though."

Grandma remarked, "I just hope Beth will let me stay up for the study tomorrow night." Grandma smiled at Beth.

Beth answered, "If you are feeling well tomorrow, we can allow at least an hour." Beth smiled back. "Anyway, if we leave your door open you can hear everything that is said."

Grandma turned to Frank, "Maybe you could give Brother Owens a list of my questions and he could be ready to talk about them first. I want to know about the Judgment in the first century. Who was judged? The dead? The living? The Old Covenant?"

"Yes," said Becca, "and I want to know if we are judged when we die?"

Joe had not taken a bite of his dinner for some time as he was listening to the comments being made. Noticing his silence, Beth asked, "Joe, are you all right?"

"What are you guys talking about?" asked Joe, looking at his mom.

"Some Bible questions," answered Beth. "You know we have been having a Bible study with Brother Owens."

Becca's dad spoke up, "If you are interested in what we are studying, boys, I would be glad to sit down with you and go over some things."

Jim looked up with his mouth full and looked from his mom to his dad with an expression on his face that implied, 'I didn't say anything', but Joe said, "All right, yeah. Maybe we could do that sometime."

Jim looked at Joe with a scowl that said 'speak for yourself and don't include me.'

However, Joe did include Jim when he said, "Jim and I would like that." Joe smiled at Jim with raised eyebrows.

After the kitchen was cleaned, Frank brought in Bibles for his and Beth's study time together.

Dad asked, "Beth, what do you think about this first century fulfillment teaching?"

She answered, "I must admit that I am starting to understand. I see now that Christ and the apostles taught that the Second Coming was near and was to occur in that generation. I also see that the Bible uses extreme language – language like *coming on the clouds* and *the sun and moon darkened*. *Hyperbolic* is what Brother Owens calls this language when describing acts of God. Those things didn't literally happen: it is just figurative language. I also understand that God uses other nations to accomplish his goals. The Romans were the ones who literally destroyed the Temple, but God used them to do His work. I was so accustomed to thinking about the Second Coming of Christ as something I had to look forward to that I feel confused about having nothing to look forward to in the future. What does all of this mean for the generations who lived after the Second Coming? What is left for us?"

Becca, who was listening to her mother, stepped over and hugged her saying, "That's exactly how I'm feeling, too. I have always looked forward to Christ coming and taking us home to heaven. But now I see that Christ's Second Coming was a fulfillment of the promise to establish the New Covenant – the New Heavens and New Earth. He came spiritually to reign over His Kingdom – His Eternal Kingdom. We can be in that Kingdom when we put our faith in Him and obey His word. If we are in the heavenly city – the New Jerusalem – now, where will we be when we die? Is heaven still heaven?"

Dad joined Becca and Mom in the hug. "I love you both so much. Thank you for taking this spiritual journey with me. If we continue to study, I trust that we will understand more than we ever thought possible."

* * *

Becca went upstairs to do her homework while her mom and dad sat in the kitchen to study. After an hour, Becca went downstairs to get a soft drink and to call Mike. She stopped at the kitchen table to see how Mom and Dad were doing. They looked up at her as Dad asked, "Finish your homework?"

"Almost. I came down to call Mike, which reminds me of a question. Cordless phones and cell phones have been out for several years now. Do you think we could get one?"

Dad laughed, "Tired of standing in the hall?"

Mom added, "Tired of everyone hearing your conversations?"

Becca blushed and agreed, "Yeah, something like that."

Mom and Dad went back to reading and Becca asked, "Will my talking on the phone bother you?"

'Not at all," answered Dad. "Just be sure to talk loud enough for us to hear."

"Very funny, Dad," said Becca as she dialed Mike's number.

"Hello," answered Mike's dad.

"Hello, Mr. Gibbons. This is Becca. May I speak to Mike?"

"I'm sorry, Becca; he's not here right now," said Mr. Gibbons. "May I leave a note for him to call you?"

"Just say I called and that I'll see him tomorrow night. And, Mr. Gibbons, I'm glad you're coming too."

"Thank you, Becca. Goodnight."

Becca turned to go upstairs just as the doorbell rang. When Dad answered the door, Becca heard him say, "Hello, Mike." Becca headed for the door.

"May I speak to Becca for a little while?" asked Mike. "I won't be long."

"Yes, here she is now," said Dad, moving out of Becca's way.

"Hi, Mike, won't you come in?" offered Becca.

Mike whispered, "Could you get your coat and come out?"

"Sure," whispered Becca in return. Then, a little louder she said, "Mom, Dad, I'll be back soon."

Mike drove the car to the community park that was down the street from Becca's house. He got out of the car, ran around to Becca's side, and helped her out. As they walked into the park, Mike said, "I was driving home from the college library a few moments ago when I noticed something I wanted to share with you."

When they were out in a clearing, Mike said, "Look up."

Becca looked upward but wasn't sure what Mike was talking about. "What am I supposed to see?" asked Becca.

"Oh, here, turn around," instructed Mike as he turned her. When she turned, the biggest full moon that Becca had ever seen came into view. "Oh, how beautiful!" she exclaimed.

From behind, Mike surrounded her with his arms. He rested his head lightly on hers. "Like I said, I wanted to share it with you," said Mike. They stood in silence for several minutes until Mike whispered, "Becca, I think I have fallen in love with you."

Becca stood still and could not find words to express her feelings. She had been afraid things would go too fast between her and Mike, and here was Mike taking the next step. Becca struggled to hold onto her emotions, but, nevertheless, a tear rolled down her cheek and dropped onto Mike's hand. As he gently turned her around and saw her tears, a look of confusion darkened his face.

"Have I said the wrong thing?" he asked. He dropped his hands from her shoulders.

Becca grasped his shoulders, burying her face in his chest. He heard her utter a muffled 'no'. A moment later, she looked up, offering a half smile.

"What's wrong?" he asked.

When Becca had regained her composure, she asked, "Do you remember the other night when you asked where I wanted to be in ten years?"

"Yes," answered Mike.

"I am afraid that our relationship will go too fast and things will get all messed up." She paused before confessing, "I think I'm falling in love with you, too, and I don't want things to get all messed up."

"What do you mean 'all messed up'?" asked Mike.

"I don't think I want to marry until I graduate from college and," Becca paused, afraid and embarrassed to say what she meant.

"Oh," said Mike. "I get it. You're afraid I'll want too much sexually and, as you say, 'things will get all messed up'."

Becca took a chance and looked into Mike's eyes. Mike answered, "I'm sorry, I didn't mean to rush you. I just wanted to be honest with you." Mike paused, then, continued. "I think I am falling in love with you, but I promise you this: I won't ask anything from you that you don't want to give. I won't say anything about love again for at least, oh, let's say, for at least a year." Mike laughed, put his arms around Becca and lifted her off the ground with a hug. "Now, turn around and let's enjoy this moon before it's gone."

Becca turned around in Mike's arms so that she could see the moon. In a moment she calmly whispered, "Thank you."

"Come on. I had better get you home," said Mike.

"Wait a minute," said Becca. She turned to Mike, put her arms around his neck and pulled his head down to kiss him playfully. He responded, pulled her tight against him and kissed her. As he released her and they started for the car, Mike said, "You don't make it easy on a guy."

* * *

At her window that night Becca said, "Thank you, God. Thank you for my family and thank you for Mike. In Jesus' Name, Amen."

Chapter 20
Tuesday Night Number Four

Tuesday after school, Becca checked in on Grandma, who was sleeping. Becca closed the door quietly to avoid disturbing her. Becca then straightened the house, especially the kitchen, in preparation for the study group. Her mom had a casserole in the oven for the family, and had also made a sheet cake for their guests tonight. Becca turned her attention to the table. Mr. Gibbons was expected to join them tonight and, hopefully, Mrs. Gibbons would, too.

Becca went to the hall closet to get an extra leaf for the table. Expanding the table, however, made moving around in the kitchen more difficult, so Mom suggested that the study be moved to the living room. The living room had a sofa, loveseat and one chair; in addition, a couple of chairs could be brought in from the kitchen.

Becca's mom left for a quick trip to the store to get hot rolls to go with tonight's dinner. Becca returned the table leaf to the closet and got out the vacuum cleaner to clean in the living room. She heard Grandma's voice weakly call from the bedroom, "Beth, is that you?"

"It's Becca, Grandma. I'm sorry I woke you with all this noise," said Becca as she entered Grandma's room. "Mom's gone to the store." Becca sat on the edge of Grandma's bed. "How are you feeling, Grandma?"

"I'm feeling a little dizzy, dear. The room spins around when I try to sit up, but I must get to the bathroom. I'm sorry to have to ask you, but do you think you can help me?"

"Sure, Grandma," said Becca, but she was worried that she wasn't doing the right thing. She reasoned that, if Grandma was dizzy, maybe she shouldn't get her out of the bed at all. Becca asked, "Grandma, are you sure it is OK to get up when you are dizzy?"

"I have to, Dear," said Grandma. "Please help me." Grandma added, "I feel better if I keep my eyes shut, so you tell me when and where to step."

Thankfully, Grandma was a small, thin woman. Becca found it easy enough to help her, yet she breathed a sigh of relief once Grandma was back in bed.

"Thank you, Dear," said Grandma. "I hope I am feeling better tonight: I don't want to miss our study."

Becca got Grandma a fresh glass of water and helped her settle comfortably again. Becca returned to the living room where she vacuumed, dusted and straightened everything.

* * *

Grandma did not come to the table for dinner, stating that she was saving her strength to come to the Bible study. Becca took a small serving of casserole to Grandma in her room. Grandma ate so slowly that, by the time she was finished, Mike and his dad had arrived. Becca could hear Dad visiting with them in the living room. Becca returned Grandma's dishes to the kitchen just as her mom finished putting things away.

As Becca started for the living room, her mom stopped her. "Becca, I need your help with Grandma."

Becca and Beth helped Grandma to the bathroom. After a few moments of helping Grandma into a fresh dress and brushing her hair,

Mom stepped out to tell Dad that Grandma was ready. Dad appeared at the bathroom door with a wheel chair. Becca could see that Grandma was not happy with the idea of needing a wheel chair.

Frank also saw the look on his mom's face and said, "Now, Mom, it's only on loan until you're better and we'll only use it on longer trips. So it is either this or I'm going to pick you up and carry you!"

Grandma agreed, but sighed, "I don't call going to the living room 'a longer trip'." As Dad wheeled Grandma to the living room, Grandma remembered, "I need my Bible." Becca went back to get it.

By the time Becca arrived in the living room, everyone was seated. Mike and his dad had taken the love seat, Brother Owens was in the chair, and Mom and Dad were seated on the sofa. Becca chose to sit on the floor beside Grandma's wheel chair.

Brother Owens welcomed everyone, saying how glad he was that Mr. Gibbons had joined them and how he hoped that Grandma Elliott was feeling better. Brother Owens continued, "I don't know exactly where to begin tonight. We have a new member of our study group and we also had a class Sunday morning that two of our group were not able to attend."

Mr. Gibbons assured Brother Owens that Mike had studied with him, bringing him up-to-date. Becca's mom added that Becca had shared with her and Grandma the scriptures that had been covered in Sunday's class.

Becca's dad spoke up, "Brother Owens, may we begin tonight by asking you some of the questions that we have?"

Brother Owens agreed, "Yes, that will be fine."

Frank turned to his mom and said, "Mom, why don't you go first."

Grandma smiled and began, "Please explain about the Resurrection. Were the dead raised physically or is the Resurrection only a spiritual resurrection out of the Old Covenant into the New Covenant?"

Brother Owens began, "I believe that there are several aspects to the Resurrection. Prior to Christ's resurrection, men had been physically dying for hundreds of years. Even if they had tried to be holy, they were not perfect and died with sins on their record. Christ's blood reached both ways: back in time and forward. First of all, let's talk about those who had physically died before Christ's resurrection. In several scriptures the Bible talks about the 'land of the dead', Hades. I have a list of scriptures about Hades here." Brother Owens took several index cards out of his pocket and found the one on Hades. He began assigning scriptures, "Mike, please get Luke 16:22 & 23. Mr. Gibbons, find Psalms 16:10. Mr. Elliott, Acts 2:27-31. Mrs. Elliott, please get Hosea 13:14 and Becca, Eph. 4:8-9."

"Mike, will you begin with your scripture?"

Mike read,

> *"Luke 16:22-23 So it was that the beggar died, and was carried by the angels to Abraham's bosom. The rich man also died and was buried. And being in torment in Hades, he lifted up his eyes and saw Abraham afar off, and Lazarus in his bosom."*

Brother Owens commented, "I'm sure everyone recognizes the story of the rich man and Lazarus. When the rich man died, he went to the land of the dead, Hades. Mr. Gibbons, read your scripture, please."

Mr. Gibbons read,

> *"Ps 16:10 For You will not leave my soul in Sheol, Nor will You allow Your Holy One to see corruption."*

"And Mr. Elliott."

> *"Acts 2:27 For You will not leave my soul in Hades, Nor will You allow Your Holy One to see corruption."*

"The scripture which Frank read," began Brother Owens, "is a quote by Peter on the Day of Pentecost of the prophecy John read from

Psalms. Of course, it is about Christ. Christ would not remain in the land of the dead but would be resurrected. All the people who had died up until this time were held captive in Hades because of their sins. The Old Testament had prophesied that the Messiah would rescue or raise them from their graves – that is, from the land of the dead. Beth, would you read Hosea 13:14, please?"

Beth read,

"I will ransom them from the power of the grave; I will redeem them from death. O Death, I will be your plagues! O Grave, I will be your destruction!

Pity is hidden from My eyes."

"Thank you, Beth, and while you are in Hosea, would you also read Hosea 6:1-2?" asked Brother Owens.

Beth read,

"Come, and let us return to the LORD; For He has torn, but He will heal us; He has stricken, but He will bind us up. After two days He will revive us;

On the third day He will raise us up, That we may live in His sight."

Brother Owens began, "Israel knew that the Messiah would Resurrect them. The question still remains: when did this happen and what is the manner of this Resurrection? Does the scripture speak of physical bodies coming out the ground and walking around, or does it refer to their souls being taken from the land of the dead, judged and assigned their eternal abode? Let's see if we can answer the first question of when this happened? Becca, will you read Eph. 4:8-9?"

Becca read,

"Therefore He says: "When He ascended on high, He led captivity captive, And gave gifts to men." (Now this, "He ascended" — what does it mean but that He also first descended into the lower parts of the

earth? He who descended is also the One who ascended far above all the heavens, that He might fill all things.)"

Brother Owens asked Mike to be prepared to read I Corinthians 15:51-57 and then continued, "After Jesus ascended into heaven, He sent the Holy Spirit to guide the apostles. Through the power of the Holy Spirit, the apostles gave spiritual gifts to men – gifts like the ability to prophesy, speak in tongues, and heal the sick. Also, included in this verse is the concept of 'leading of captivity captive'. In other words, he was victorious over the power of death to hold the souls of men. Now, at this point, I must say it is difficult to understand the exact 'when' of the resurrection of the dead. It is possible that those who were judged faithful were taken to heaven with Christ at his ascension. In Revelation 6:9 and 20:5 we read about the souls of the martyrs beneath the altar crying out for their vindication. And, possibly, the rest of the dead were not released from their captivity until Christ's Second Coming. Mike read I Corinthians 15:51-57."

Mike read,

"Behold, I show you a mystery; We shall not all sleep, but we shall all be changed, In a moment, in the twinkling of an eye, at the last trump: for the trumpet shall sound, and the dead shall be raised incorruptible, and we shall be changed. For this corruptible must put on incorruption, and this mortal must put on immortality. So when this corruptible shall have put on incorruption, and this mortal shall have put on immortality, then shall be brought to pass the saying that is written, Death is swallowed up in victory. O death, where is thy sting? O grave, where is thy victory? The sting of death is sin; and the strength of sin is the law. But thanks be to God, which giveth us the victory through our Lord Jesus Christ."

Brother Owens continued, "This passage in I Corinthians says that the *Victory over Death* is at the sounding of the last trumpet. Now, the

Coming of the Lord in the clouds is not so that people can see him with their eyes, as many of us have been taught. Rather, it is the spiritual Coming of Christ against Jerusalem and the ending of God's Covenant with Israel. It is the Coming of Christ as the victorious King in His Kingdom. So, for the people who had died prior to Christ's coming, I believe they were brought out of the land of the dead and assigned their eternal reward during this time period. Either at His ascension or at His Second Coming, the land of the dead was emptied." Brother Owens took a breath and smiled at the group. "Do you have any questions about the dead prior to Christ's coming before I discuss those who were alive at Christ's coming?"

Grandma spoke up, "You have already cleared up a couple of my questions. Please teach on before I am sent off to bed."

Becca's dad asked, "Are you doing OK, Mom?"

Grandma smiled and said, "I think I will stay a while longer, son."

Brother Owens continued, "There is another aspect of the resurrection besides the release of the people from Hades. What about the ones who were alive at Christ's coming? Well, there are two groups of concern: the Jews who had rejected Christ as the Messiah and those who believed in him. First, let's consider the Jews who were alive but had rejected Jesus as the Christ. At the Coming of Christ in the Destruction of Jerusalem, thousands of them died literally; but whether they died physically or survived, they were now considered spiritually dead. And what about all the Christians, both Jew and Gentile, who believed in Christ? The scripture that Mike read from Corinthians said that those who were alive were changed – changed in a twinkling of an eye. Changed how? Under the old system, the Old Law, the people were not allowed in the Holy of Holies of the Temple. Thus, they were not allowed into the Presence of God. By contrast, in the New Covenant, in the New Heavens and the New Earth, we *are* in the presence of God. Frank, will you find Hebrews 4:14-16?"

Frank read,

"Seeing then that we have a great High Priest who has passed through the heavens, Jesus the Son of God, let us hold fast our confession. For we do not have a High Priest who cannot sympathize with our weaknesses, but was in all points tempted as we are, yet without sin. Let us therefore come boldly to the throne of grace, that we may obtain mercy and find grace to help in time of need."

"Becca, will you get Ephesians 2:12-21, please?" asked Brother Owens. "I want to end this question about the resurrection with this point. The promises of the Messiah were made first to the Jews, but not to the Jews only. The Gentiles were to be brought into the promises, also. They were raised out of *sin death* into *life in Christ* the same way the Jewish Christians were, through the resurrection of baptism. The passage that Becca is going to read is longer than the others which we have read tonight, but it is a very good summary of the joy and victory for the Gentiles who believed in Christ during the first century and those who continue to believe in Christ even today. This scripture applies to them and to us, because we are Gentiles."

Becca read,

"Ephesians 2:12-21: Therefore remember that you, once Gentiles in the flesh — who are called Uncircumcision by what is called the Circumcision made in the flesh by hands — that at that time you were without Christ, being aliens from the commonwealth of Israel and strangers from the covenants of promise, having no hope and without God in the world. But now in Christ Jesus you who once were far off have been brought near by the blood of Christ. For He Himself is our peace, who has made both one, and has broken down the middle wall of separation, having abolished in His flesh the enmity, that is, the law of commandments contained in ordinances, so as to create in Himself one new man from the two, thus making peace, and that He might reconcile them both to God in one body through the cross,

thereby putting to death the enmity. And He came and preached peace to you who were afar off and to those who were near. For through Him we both have access by one Spirit to the Father. Now, therefore, you are no longer strangers and foreigners, but fellow citizens with the saints and members of the household of God, having been built on the foundation of the apostles and prophets, Jesus Christ Himself being the chief cornerstone, in whom the whole building, being fitted together, grows into a holy temple in the Lord, in whom you also are being built together for a dwelling place of God in the Spirit."

Becca was impacted by the scripture she had just read. She realized that it was speaking not only to the people who accepted Christ in the first century but to her, also. She looked around the room and she could see that everyone was touched by the good news of Resurrection – being spiritually raised out of sin death into the very Presence of God.

Brother Owens turned in his Bible and began to read (Romans 6:4-14),

'Therefore we were buried with Him through baptism into death, that just as Christ was raised from the dead by the glory of the Father, even so we also should walk in newness of life. For if we have been united together in the likeness of His death, certainly we also shall be in the likeness of His resurrection, knowing this, that our old man was crucified with Him, that the body of sin might be done away with, that we should no longer be slaves of sin. For he who has died has been freed from sin. Now if we died with Christ, we believe that we shall also live with Him, knowing that Christ, having been raised from the dead, dies no more. Death no longer has dominion over Him. For the death that He died, He died to sin once for all; but the life that He lives, He lives to God. Likewise you also, reckon yourselves to be dead indeed to sin, but alive to God in Christ Jesus our Lord. Therefore do not let sin reign in your mortal body, that you should obey it in its lusts. And

do not present your members as instruments of unrighteousness to sin, but present yourselves to God as being alive from the dead, and your members as instruments of righteousness to God. For sin shall not have dominion over you, for you are not under law but under grace.'

"Paul is not speaking of a resurrection of our mortal bodies someday in the future. He is talking about the Resurrection we have in Christ. As we live our daily lives, we are sons and daughters of God, abiding in His presence."

Becca asked softly, "And when we die physically?"

Grandma answered, "We leave this mortal body behind and continue to live in God's presence. Thank you, Brother Owens. May God bless you for helping me to understand." Grandma smiled and said, "Frank, will you help me to my room?"

Becca and her dad helped Grandma to her room. Becca helped Grandma into a comfortable nightgown. As Grandma lay back, she said, "Becca, thank you for making this study happen. It is so good to know the full joy of the gospel and to live – and die – without fear."

Becca was unable to speak. She was so overwhelmed by the study that she could not bear to think of Grandma's dying at the same time. She fought back tears as she kissed Grandma good-night.

When she returned to the kitchen, Mom and Dad were getting cake and drinks for everyone. Becca buried her head in her dad's chest.

"Hey, Sis, what's wrong?" asked her dad.

Becca murmured, "I don't like to hear Grandma talk about dying."

Her dad patted her on the back for a moment, then pushed her back so that he could look into her face as he smiled at her. "Grandma's going to be all right. Dry your tears and help your mom with the cake and drinks. I'm going to go tell Grandma good-night."

Becca brightened and began serving cake to the guests in the living room. Mike's dad was looking very concerned. Becca and Mike exchanged questioning glances.

Mr. Gibbons said, "Brother Owens, I am starting to understand what you are teaching and it doesn't sound like heresy to me. It is really making a lot of sense. I understand some scriptures now that I never understood before. But..." Mr. Gibbons paused, "but I have to be honest with you. There are some who are calling meetings to discuss what they are calling heresy... and your job is on the line."

Brother Owens thought a moment, before replying, "I understand, John, and I appreciate your honesty, but I can't do anything different than what I'm doing. I will preach what I believe the Word of God says. I don't think the Bible contradicts itself, and I don't think the Bible teaches two different things. The Bible has one message and one truth. When Christ said He was coming in the lifetime of the people to whom He was speaking, I believe He did what He promised. And as we read tonight, I don't believe the Coming of Christ with Resurrection and Judgment in the first century lessens the power of the gospel for us in any way. Christ's Kingdom is eternal and people centuries from now can enter the Kingdom through faith and baptism to live in the Presence of God in this life and to continue with God eternally. I can't preach it any other way."

Becca's dad had stepped back into the room. Becca could see the concern in his expression. "Excuse me," he said. "Grandma is having severe pain in her chest, so we've called an ambulance for her. Brother Owens, Grandma would like to speak to you."

Chapter 21
In The Presence of God

The paramedics allowed Mr. Elliott to ride in the ambulance as they rushed his mom to the hospital. Brother Owens drove the rest of the family in his car, while Mike and his dad followed in their car. By the time the group arrived at the hospital, Dad was consulting with the emergency room doctor. When he saw the group enter, he approached them.

Several spoke at the same time, "How is she?"

"The paramedics said that her blood pressure was low and confirmed that her heart beat is irregular. The doctors are taking her to the ICU and are trying to get her blood pressure stabilized. They have called in a cardiac specialist, and Grandma's doctor is on his way, too. I want Beth to come with me to the ICU. The rest of you may wait in the ICU family room. Brother Owens, Mr. Gibbons, and Mike, thank you for coming." A nurse showed Dad and Mom to the ICU while the rest of the group stopped at the waiting area.

Becca had been brave up until this point, but she could no longer hold back the tears. She turned her head into Mike's shoulder and sobbed. Brother Owens sat with Joe and Jim, who were sitting in stunned silence as Becca's sobs further increased their distress. Mr. Gibbons quickly brought a glass of water for Becca. Noticing the fearful expressions on her brothers' faces, she was able to calm her emotions enough to offer comfort to them.

"I'm sorry," she said as she tried to wipe away the tears.

Attempting to console both her and the boys, Brother Owens said, "Don't apologize. Crying is allowed and completely understandable." He continued, "I'm hopeful the doctors will be able to help her, but I will offer a prayer for her if you wish." Becca and Joe both nodded their heads affirmatively.

Brother Owens prayed, "Dear Heavenly Father, we pray to you tonight for our sister in Christ, for the grandmother of Becca, Joe and Jim. Father, please, be with her and help the doctors who care for her. Father, if it be Thy will, we ask you to let us keep this wonderful woman here with us. She is a blessing to her family, to the church and to me. It is through her influence that this family has grown to be a faithful, loving Christian family. Father, if it is Thy will that she leave us, we are assured that she has an eternal home with you and that she will continue in your loving presence as she is now. In Jesus' Holy Name, Amen."

Becca rose to hug her brothers, holding on to them for several moments until Mom entered the room. Mom's eyes were also red with tears. She went immediately to Becca and the boys. As she held them, she said, "Grandma's blood pressure is starting to come up a little, but the doctors are very concerned." Mom paused to take a sip of the water that Mr. Gibbons offered her. She continued, "They said that we should call other family members who would want to be here." Turning to Mike and Mr. Gibbons, she said, "I'm sorry to have to ask you, but would you mind going back to the house to find my address book? It's in the table by the phone in the hall. If you will call the ICU desk, I can tell you who needs a call. If you can call them from our home phone, I would appreciate it very much."

Brother Owens volunteered, "John, my wife can help you with that. I'll give her a call and have her meet you at the Elliott's home."

Mom smiled as she patted her tears with a tissue, "That would really help a lot. Thank you." Mom handed the house keys to Mr. Gibbons.

As Mr. Gibbons turned to go, Mike asked, "If it's all right, Dad, I would like to stay here with Becca."

"Sure, son, that's fine."

Mom went back to the ICU as the group sat to wait.

* * *

After an hour had passed, Mr. Elliott came into the waiting room just as Mr. Gibbons and Mrs. Owens returned from making the phone calls. As the group stood to hear Dad's news, Becca went into her dad's arms.

He began, "She's stable right now, but her heart is really weak and she is still unconscious."

"Unconscious?" Becca asked.

"Yes," said Dad. "She fell into unconsciousness in the ambulance. The doctors say we will probably have to make the decision whether or not to put her on life support." He paused. "Having gone through this situation with Mom when Dad died, I know she would say no to life support." Dad sighed and continued, "But I think I would like to try life support until the doctors have tried to make some improvement in her condition. After that, if she doesn't regain consciousness or she can't continue without life support, I'm afraid we will have to let her go." Dad held Becca and the boys in his arms for a long consoling hug. Then he looked across to Mr. Gibbons and Mrs. Owens, "Were you able to contact my sister, Joan, in Marshall?"

"Yes," said Mrs. Owens. "She's on her way."

"Good," said Dad. Then, trying to smile for his children, he said, "You guys should probably go home and get to bed."

Becca shook her head, "No, Dad. Don't ask us to go. Let us wait here with you."

Dad nodded that they could stay. He rubbed his face in his hands and looked at the group. "Thank you all for being here."

* * *

Joan and her family arrived at 12:30 A.M. Joan went in with Frank to see their mother. They both returned in a few minutes. Dad said, "Grandma's heart beat is very weak. The doctors have put her on life support. The doctors said you may step in to see her if you want to. Dad took Becca and the boys in first. Becca kissed her grandma's cheek as she had done so many times. The boys stood silently looking at Grandma until Joe reached his hand out and laid it on Grandma's arm. Jim did the same.

As they came out of the ICU and Joan went in with her girls, Mom gathered them in her arms and said, "Remember, if we must let Grandma go, she's going to be with God."

Becca thought a moment and said, "Mom, I think Grandma has been with God her whole life."

Mom was surprised at first by what Becca had said. Then she smiled and said, "Yes, I think you are right. Grandma has walked with her Savior and lived in the presence of God her whole life. Death will not change that."

Grandma passed from this mortal life at 2:30 A.M.

Chapter 22
A New Fellowship

Becca was happy and sad about the same event. Even though she was deeply grieved over the loss of her grandma, Becca was also happy because she could picture in her mind Grandma's being reunited with Grandpa. Because Mom knew how difficult Grandma's death was for Becca, she located a picture that had been taken of Grandma and Grandpa a few months before Grandpa's death. She had the photograph enlarged and framed for Becca's room. Seeing it above her bed made Becca feel as if Grandma and Grandpa were both smiling down on her.

When Dad and Joan cleaned out Grandma's room, they agreed that Dad would keep Grandpa's Bible. Joan took the quilt and hairbrush set. Since the pages of the photo album were deteriorating, the pictures were removed from the sheets and put in a box for storage. They sent the large picture of Grandpa to a photography studio to have copies made and framed for both Joan and Frank and the original put in secure storage.

* * *

Sunday morning, the weather was clear and cold. Mike was waiting for Becca on the front steps of the church building, and entered with her family. Even though many people from the congregation had expressed their condolences to Dad and the family at Grandma's funeral, many continued to offer kind words to them as they entered the church building. As they made their way though the foyer, Becca heard her name spoken softly behind her. When she turned around, she saw Jenny and Ben. Ben looked really nervous but was able to say, "I'm sorry about your grandmother." Jenny gave Becca a hug but was unable to say anything.

"Thank you, Ben," said Becca. "That's nice of you to say. Thank you, Jenny."

Ben and Jenny smiled in return and moved away to go to their class. Becca and Mike attended the adult class with their parents.

When class started, Brother Owens asked everyone to turn to Matthew 24. He took the time to read the entire chapter."

"1 Then Jesus went out and departed from the temple, and His disciples came up to show Him the buildings of the temple. 2 And Jesus said to them, "Do you not see all these things? Assuredly, I say to you, not one stone shall be left here upon another, that shall not be thrown down."

3 Now as He sat on the Mount of Olives, the disciples came to Him privately, saying, "Tell us, when will these things be? And what will be the sign of Your coming, and of the end of the age?"

4 And Jesus answered and said to them: "Take heed that no one deceives you. 5 For many will come in My name, saying, 'I am the Christ,' and will deceive many. 6 And you will hear of wars and rumors of wars. See that you are not troubled; for all these things must come to pass, but the end is not yet. 7 For nation will rise against nation, and kingdom against kingdom. And there will be famines, pestilences, and earthquakes in various places. 8 All these are the beginning of sorrows.

9 "Then they will deliver you up to tribulation and kill you, and you will be hated by all nations for My name's sake. 10 And then many will be offended, will betray one another, and will hate one another.

11 Then many false prophets will rise up and deceive many. 12 And because lawlessness will abound, the love of many will grow cold. 13 But he who endures to the end shall be saved. 14 And this gospel of the kingdom will be preached in all the world as a witness to all the nations, and then the end will come.

15 "Therefore when you see the 'abomination of desolation,' spoken of by Daniel the prophet, standing in the holy place" (whoever reads, let him understand), 16 "then let those who are in Judea flee to the mountains. 17 Let him who is on the housetop not go down to take anything out of his house. 18 And let him who is in the field not go back to get his clothes. 19 But woe to those who are pregnant and to those who are nursing babies in those days! 20 And pray that your flight may not be in winter or on the Sabbath. 21 For then there will be great tribulation, such as has not been since the beginning of the world until this time, no, nor ever shall be. 22 And unless those days were shortened, no flesh would be saved; but for the elect's sake those days will be shortened.

23 "Then if anyone says to you, 'Look, here is the Christ!' or 'There!' do not believe it. 24 For false christs and false prophets will rise and show great signs and wonders to deceive, if possible, even the elect. 25 See, I have told you beforehand.

26 "Therefore if they say to you, 'Look, He is in the desert!' do not go out; or 'Look, He is in the inner rooms!' do not believe it. 27 For as the lightning comes from the east and flashes to the west, so also will the coming of the Son of Man be. 28 For wherever the carcass is, there the eagles will be gathered together.

29 "Immediately after the tribulation of those days the sun will be darkened, and the moon will not give its light; the stars will fall from heaven, and the powers of the heavens will be shaken. 30 Then the sign of the Son of Man will appear in heaven, and then all the tribes of the earth will mourn, and they will see the Son of Man coming on the clouds of heaven with power and great glory. 31 And He will send His

angels with a great sound of a trumpet, and they will gather together His elect from the four winds, from one end of heaven to the other.

32 "Now learn this parable from the fig tree: When its branch has already become tender and puts forth leaves, you know that summer is near. 33 So you also, when you see all these things, know that it is near — at the doors! 34 Assuredly, I say to you, this generation will by no means pass away till all these things take place. 35 Heaven and earth will pass away, but My words will by no means pass away.

36 "But of that day and hour no one knows, not even the angels of heaven, but My Father only. 37 But as the days of Noah were, so also will the coming of the Son of Man be. 38 For as in the days before the flood, they were eating and drinking, marrying and giving in marriage, until the day that Noah entered the ark, 39 and did not know until the flood came and took them all away, so also will the coming of the Son of Man be. 40 Then two men will be in the field: one will be taken and the other left. 41 Two women will be grinding at the mill: one will be taken and the other left. 42 Watch therefore, for you do not know what hour your Lord is coming. 43 But know this, that if the master of the house had known what hour the thief would come, he would have watched and not allowed his house to be broken into. 44 Therefore you also be ready, for the Son of Man is coming at an hour you do not expect.

45 "Who then is a faithful and wise servant, whom his master made ruler over his household, to give them food in due season? 46 Blessed is that servant whom his master, when he comes, will find so doing. 47 Assuredly, I say to you that he will make him ruler over all his goods. 48 But if that evil servant says in his heart, 'My master is delaying his coming,' 49 and begins to beat his fellow servants, and to eat and drink with the drunkards, 50 the master of that servant will come on a day when he is not looking for him and at an hour that he is not aware of, 51 and will cut him in two and appoint him his portion with the hypocrites. There shall be weeping and gnashing of teeth."

Then Brother Owens asked, "Did Jesus say that his Second Coming would be in that generation?" Becca's dad motioned for her and Mike not to speak, so the room remained quiet.

Brother Owens asked another question, "If Jesus did return, and I mean that in a spiritual way, in that generation, what further questions would be raised in your mind? Would there be conflict with other scriptures?"

A voice from the back of the room asked, "Are you saying, Mr. Owens, that you believe that the Second Coming of Christ happened in the first century and, therefore, there is not another Coming of the Lord at which He will resurrect and judge the world?"

The room was silent for a moment before Brother Owens spoke, "Yes, I believe that the Second Coming of Christ, the Resurrection and the Judgment happened in the first century A.D.. What that means to us is that all spiritual promises have been kept and that eternal life for all who are obedient to God is assured."

The speaker from the back of the room was Mr. Collin. Mr. Collin said, "Mr. Gibbons, Mr. Phillips, could I speak to you in the foyer?"

When the men had left the room, Brother Owens asked, "Does anyone have a question?"

Becca's dad stood and turned so he could address the class. "My family and I have been studying with Brother Owens. I have learned much about the scriptures that I didn't understand before." Dad paused, turned to look at Becca and Beth, and then continued, "I only speak for myself when I say that I, too, believe that Christ's Second Coming occurred in the first century. Matthew 5:17-18 says that *all* had to be fulfilled before the Old Law could pass away. The Old Heavens and Earth had to pass away to allow the coming of the New Heavens and New Earth of the Messiah – not the literal, physical heaven and earth, but the spiritual heaven and earth of the covenants. Christ's Kingdom, in which He now reigns, is eternal. Men from now on can gain eternal life in His Kingdom through faith and obedience. My mother came to a full understanding of this before her death. If what Brother Owens is teaching is truth – and I believe it is – then that means that Mom has passed into her eternal home with God. She is not in the 'land of the dead' waiting for a future resurrection of her body."

The class members were looking at Dad and at Brother Owens. Dad looked around for a moment, then turned and sat down.

The door to the classroom opened and Mr. Collin said, "Mr. Owens we would like to speak to you, please."

After Brother Owens left the room, the class members turned to talk among themselves. Becca asked Dad, "What's happening?" Mike leaned forward to hear.

"Well, I'm afraid it is not good. Mr. Collin will probably call for a vote of the leaders. Since Mike's dad is the only one of the leaders who has studied the issue, I suspect that the vote will be to terminate Brother Owens' employment as our minister. Did you hear how Mr. Collin called him *Mr. Owens* instead of *Brother Owens*? The leaders will take the stand that they cannot allow heresy to be taught and, if it were heresy, they would be right."

"Do you mean they are going to fire Brother Owens?" asked Becca as the tears started in her eyes.

"We'll probably know soon," said Dad.

"Can't you do something about it, Dad?" asked Becca as an unexpected anger grew within her.

Dad located the meeting between the leaders and Brothers Owens in the church office. Mr. Collin was in the process of telling Frank that this was a leaders' meeting and that he should leave, when Brother Owens said, "Brother Elliott, don't worry about me. We just have a few details to work out about my severance pay and I'll be through here."

Mr. Collin addressed Frank again, "Mr. Elliott, if you believe what this man has been teaching, you need to reconsider. You are putting your soul in jeopardy and need to repent. This doctrine is heresy."

At this point, John Gibbons spoke, "Let's not get carried away, Brother Collin. Let's just finish here and let everybody cool down."

Dad waited outside the door for a few minutes until Brother Owens came out. "Thank you, Brother Elliott, for coming to my aid. I need to get my wife out of the second grade room where she is teaching so that we can leave."

"I'll call you this afternoon," said Dad as Brother Owens went down the hall.

The announcement in the church service was short and to the point. 'Because he believed and taught the doctrine that Christ's Second Coming happened in 70 A.D. and that we do not now have the hope of resurrection, Mr. Owens has been dismissed as the minister of this congregation.' After the song leader led several songs and communion was observed, morning services were dismissed. Dad scolded Jim on the way home when he overheard him say that he wished services were that short all the time.

Becca, her dad and her mom sat down at the kitchen table. Dad began, "I told Brother Owens I would call him this afternoon."

"What will he do, Dad? Will he move away?" asked Becca.

"I don't know, Sis," answered her dad with a sigh.

"What will we do?" asked Becca.

"What do you mean?" asked Mom.

"If I believe that Christ's Second Coming is past, as Brother Owens taught, will the church ask me to leave, too?" asked Becca.

"I think there will be pressure put on us to repent of that belief. Mr. Collin indicted that to me this morning," said Dad. "I'm sure if you try to talk about or teach others your belief, you will be asked to leave."

Mom was upset, "I knew something like this would happen?"

Dad looked at Mom, "Where are you in all of this, Beth? What do you believe now?"

Mom turned her thoughts inward with her eyes downcast. Finally, she raised her head, "I believe that all has been fulfilled, including the

Second Coming." Mom paused, sighed and continued, "And I feel disconnected without a church home."

Becca asked, "When the Cedarvale church split over this issue, where did the people go, who believe as we do? Where do they meet for worship?"

"I don't know," said her Dad. "I think I will see if I can get Brother Owens on the phone now."

When Dad returned from the hall, he said, "I think we need to go over to the Owens' house. His wife is taking this pretty hard and they have some hard decisions to make. We need to let them know that they have friends who care."

As Becca stood, she said, "I'm going to call Mike."

When Becca told Mike that they were going to the Owens' home, he said he would meet her there. Fifteen minutes later, Becca's family was seated in the Owens' living room. Beth was consoling Mrs. Owens and promising to help her any way possible when the door bell rang. Not only Mike, but Mr. and Mrs. Gibbons, entered to offer consolation.

Mr. Gibbons said, "Brother Owens, I want you know that I did not vote to have you dismissed. I'm sorry that this happened. I'm sorry that the others didn't study the issue more fully before rushing to judgment."

Brother Owens shook Mr. Gibbons' hand, "Thank you, John. I appreciate that."

"What will you do?" asked Mr. Gibbons.

"Well, I suppose I will look for another preaching position." Then, more seriously, he continued, "However, I don't have much hope that one will be offered to me, considering the belief I hold. I have a teaching degree. I may have to take a teaching job and try to preach on the side."

Mr. Gibbons continued, "When I went to the Cedarville congregation a few weeks ago, one of the leaders there mentioned that the group who believe the 70 A.D. heresy – as he called it – was meeting in each others' homes."

"Yes," said Brother Owens, "I've met a couple of those families. The preacher who was there had to move away to support his family, leaving the Cedarvale group to study on their own. They heard that I was teaching the same thing and asked me if I could study with them.

Becca's dad spoke up, "I need to get to know them. My family may want to start worshipping with them, too."

Mr. Gibbons continued, "That's what I was thinking. If those of us who support you join with the group at Cedarville, maybe we could at least pay you for part time preaching until our numbers grow."

Brother Owens asked Mr. Gibbons, "John, do you mean you are willing to leave the congregation where you are a leader?"

"Leader or not, I want to be with a congregation of people who are not afraid to admit when they are wrong and are willing to study in search of the truth."

Dad stepped over to shake John's hand but ended up hugging him instead.

Mr. Gibbons said, "Frank and Becca, I want to thank you for causing this study to happen." Turning to his son he said, "Mike, thank you for bugging me until I was shamed into studying." Mike crossed the room to hug his dad.

Mr. Elliott turned to Brother Owens, "Do you think you can help me get in touch with the group from Cedarvale?"

"Of course," said Brother Owens as he handed the phone numbers for two of the Cedarvale families to Frank and offered, "Please use our phone."

Frank spoke on the phone for just a couple of minutes. When he returned to the group, he had the address of where the Cedarvale group was meeting tonight. "I spoke to a Mr. Albright. He said that they were meeting tonight for a fellowship supper and devotional. He said that there would be plenty of food and that we should come."

Mrs. Gibbons was sitting next to Mrs. Owens and Beth. Beth quietly asked Mrs. Gibbons, "Linda, how are you doing?"

Mrs. Gibbons smiled, "Do you mean, do I agree with the 70 A.D. fulfillment? I don't know. But I appreciate that my husband is willing to study an issue before calling someone a heretic. So I guess I had better study the issue before I make up my mind."

* * *

That evening the Owens, Gibbons, and Elliott families were welcomed by a group of seven Cedarvale families. The fellowship was genuine. An instant bond and atmosphere of understanding flowed through them all.

The prayer offered that night by the entire group was for Brother Owens and his wife. The man who led the prayer said, "Father, if it is thy will, please let Brother Owens and his wife stay in this area. We need him to guide our study and strengthen our knowledge. He will be a blessing to us. Help us, Father, to find the way to support him as he does Your work. In Jesus' Name, Amen."

* * *

The Owens did stay with this new congregation of God's people. Brother Owens and his wife both secured jobs with school systems in the area. As the weeks went by, other members of the congregation where the Elliotts and Gibbons had formerly been members called and asked to set up Bible studies. Many had been in the Sunday class with Brother Owens and wanted to learn more. After a year, four other families had joined the new congregation.

Mike and Becca continued to date. The Gibbons and the Elliott families became closer friends.

* * *

As the weeks went by, Becca would stand at her window in the evenings. The same neighborhood lay before her. The same moon and stars shone above her. However, her view of life was now different. Her life was filled with the joy of salvation. She had God's peace deep in her heart. Fear of God and death were replaced with unbounded love and assurance. Becca knew what happens to you when you die physically. Becca sensed that both Grandpa and Grandma were smiling down on her from their eternal home with God.

About the Author

Shella Fitzgerald is a native Oklahoman. From a young age, she has been an avid student of the Bible. Shella is committed to the belief that the true message of the Bible is that God has kept all His promises and has completed His plan of salvation. Because of God's completed work, mankind has within its reach forgiveness and salvation in this life and when passing from this mortal life the opportunity to continue in the presence of God for eternity. Shella writes with a subtle humor and clear story telling style that makes *Becca's Window* an easy yet endearing and profound read.